HOMEWORK S for MICROECONOMICS

to accompany

Byrns/Stone
MICROECONOMICS
Sixth Edition

Ralph T. Byrns
University of Colorado-Boulder

Gerald W. Stone
Metropolitan State College of Denver

 HarperCollins*CollegePublishers*

The authors wish to thank Professor Stephen Stageberg, *Mary Washington College*, for his diligent and speedy proofreading.

Graphs from THE ECONOMIST. Copyright © by The Economist Newspaper Group, Inc. Reprinted with permission. Further reproduction prohibited.

Homework Sets for Microeconomics to accompany Byrns/Stone, MICROECONOMICS, Sixth Edition

ISBN: 0-673-99342-6

94 95 96 97 98 9 8 7 6 5 4 3 2 1

Table of Contents

How to Answer the HomeWork Sets

Each HomeWork Set consists of 25 questions and occasionally some optional questions for you to consider. All of the answers to the 25 questions on each HomeWork Set are contained at the end of that specific HomeWork Set. Your problem, of course, is to match up the correct answer with each question.

The correct answers are set up in multiple columns of answers (*a*) through (*e*). Consider the following question and sets of answers:

The unemployment rate during the Great Depression peaked at what level (in percent)?

(*a*) 1	(*a*) point a	(*a*) inside and on the PPF
(*b*) 2	(*b*) point b	(*b*) demand decreases to D_2
(*c*) 3	(*c*) point c	(*c*) true
(*d*) 3.6	(*d*) 15	(*d*) false
(*e*) 4	(*e*) 25	(*e*) PPF_1

(*a*) 6	(*a*) Diagram A	(*a*) Q_1
(*b*) 8	(*b*) 15	(*b*) Q_0
(*c*) 10	(*c*) goods	(*c*) Q_2
(*d*) no	(*d*) inside the PPF	(*d*) Diagram D
(*e*) yes	(*e*) on the PPF	(*e*) law of decreasing costs

The correct answer is 25 percent. This answer is found in the second column (answer *e*). Thus for this question you would fill-in answer "*e*" on the answer sheet. Note that the question asked for the answer in percent, and therefore, the number 25 is sufficient.

Sometimes the answers will be numbers (like column 1), points on a diagram (like those in column 2), a diagram itself (like answer *a* in column 5 and answer *d* in column 6) or even a sentence or sentence fragment (like, among others, answers *a* and *b* in column 3). Find the correct answer (there will be only **one** correct answer to each question) and then fill-in that letter (*a*) - (*e*) on the answer sheet.

Graphs, Algebra, and Economic Analysis
(Using graphs and algebra to turn complicated circumstances into simple analysis)

Economics uses graphs and algebra as basic tools of analysis. Economists are able to analyze difficult and complex problems that would be nearly impossible to dissect without these tools. With the aid of a few graphs we can examine complex issues that without them would take reams of paper to discuss. In this chapter you will learn:

- How graphs are defined and used.
- Why the unit of measurement is important.
- How to find the slope of a line and curve.
- How to use graphs without numbers.
- How to find a simple equation for a straight line.
- How to compute percentage changes.
- How to approach and analyze economic problems.

Graphs

Graphs are Functional Relationships

The typical graph depicts the relationship between two variables. Five data points for each of two variables, hours of study per week and grade (in percent) on an examination, are shown in Table 1. This tabular data is graphed in Figure 1 where the dependent variable, grade on the examination, is plotted on the vertical axis and the independent variable, hours of study, is plotted on the horizontal axis.

TABLE 1: Study Hours And Grades

Hours of Study per Week	Grades (Percent Correct)
0	20
2	40
4	60
6	80
8	100

Dependent and Independent Variables

The independent variable (X) is a variable that, when changed, causes the dependent variable to change. The dependent variable (Y) is altered as a result of changes in the independent variable. Thus, more hours of study leads to higher grades.

Direct and Inverse Relationships

The data presented in Table 1 and Figure 1 represent a direct (or positive) relationship. A direct relationship occurs when a change in the independent variable causes a similar change in the dependent variable. Increasing hours of study increase exam scores.

Conversely, an inverse relationship results when a change in the independent variable causes the opposite change in the dependent variable. An inverse relationship is shown in Figure 2, depicting the relationship between the number of check-out counters operating and the waiting time before check-out. The more counters operating the lower the wait.

Direct relationships are represented by graphs with positive slopes and inverse relationships involve graphs with negative slopes.

FIGURE 1

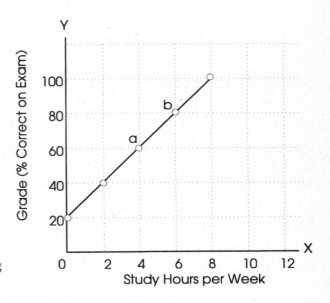

FIGURE 2

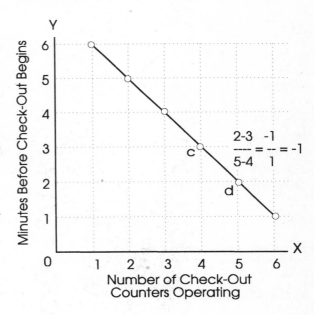

Graphs, Algebra, and Economic Analysis

Scatter Diagrams

Scatter diagrams are nothing more than two series of data plotted against each other. For example, Table 2 and Figure 3 show total personal income and total consumer spending in trillions of dollars for the U.S. for each year since 1983. Income is plotted on the horizontal (X) axis and spending is plotted on the vertical (Y) axis. A quick look at the diagram suggests that these two variables are positively related to each other. That is, a line drawn to represent the relationship would have a positive slope.

Scatter diagrams help us see the nature of the relationship between variables.

TABLE 2: Personal Income And Consumer Spending (Trillions Of Dollars)   FIGURE 3

Year	Consumer Spending	Personal Income
1983	2.258	2.863
1984	2.460	3.155
1985	2.667	3.380
1986	2.851	3.590
1987	3.052	3.802
1988	3.296	4.076
1989	3.518	4.380
1990	3.743	4.680
1991	3.887	4.834

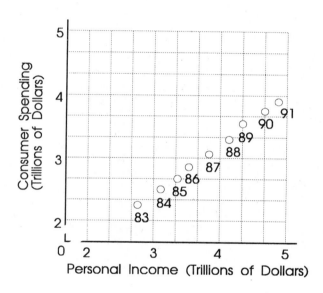

Computing the Slope of Lines and Curves

The slope of a straight line is constant along that line and is represented by the formula:

$$\frac{\text{change in dependent variable (Y)}}{\text{change in independent variable (X)}}$$

For example, the slope of the line in Figure 1 between points a and b is:

$$\frac{\text{change in Y}}{\text{change in X}} = \frac{80 - 60}{6 - 4} = \frac{20}{2} = 10$$

Every additional hour of study results in an examination score that is 10 percentage points higher. The slope is positive, thus, the relationship is direct.

The slope of the line in Figure 2 between points c and d is calculated by:

Graphs, Algebra, and Economic Analysis

$$\frac{\text{change in Y}}{\text{change in X}} = \frac{2-3}{5-4} = \frac{-1}{1} = -1$$

In Figure 2, the slope is negative and the relationship is inverse. The fewer the check-out stations operating, the longer the wait.

Units of Measurement are Important

The unit of measurement on each axis is important. For example, the line in Figure 4 appears to have the same slope as Figure 2, but a closer inspection will reveal that this conclusion is erroneous. Between points e and f the computed slope is -2.5 [(10-15)/(10-8) = -5/2 = -2.5]. Always check the units measured on each axis when you compute the slope.

Finding the Slope of a Curve

The slope of a curve varies at all points along the curve. To find the slope at any point on a curve, draw a tangent to the curve (a line that just touches the curve) and then determine the slope of that tangent. Figure 5 illustrates this process. For point a, the tangent has a slope of 3.13 while at point b the tangent has a slope of 9.

Marginal = Slope

Economists often talk about marginal this and marginal that. The term "marginal" means the change in Y associated with an additional unit of X. This is just another way of looking at slope.

FIGURE 4

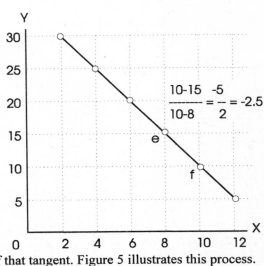

FIGURE 5

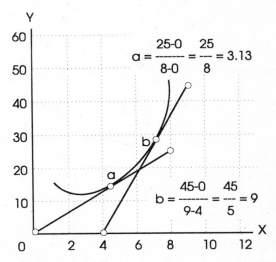

Maximum and Minimum Points

FIGURE 6

Curves reach a local maximum or minimum point when the slope of the curve is zero. In Figure 6, curve A reaches its lowest point at X = 3 and Y = 3. At that point, the tangent to point a has a slope of 0; a change in X yields no change in Y. Similarly, curve B reaches its maximum at X = 3 and Y = 6 and the slope of the tangent to point b = 0.

Notice that both curves A and B have portions of their curves that have positive and negative slopes.

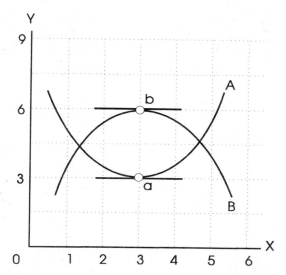

45° Reference Lines

FIGURE 7

Economists often use a 45° reference line. At all points along this 45° reference line (shown in Figure 7) X = Y. Given a second line, A, comparisons to this reference line are quick and easy. For all values below 5 (point a), Y > X and for values above 5, Y < X. Only at point a does Y = X.

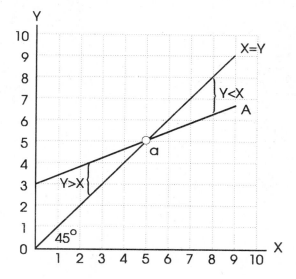

Graphs, Algebra, and Economic Analysis

Ceteris Paribus and Shifts in Curves

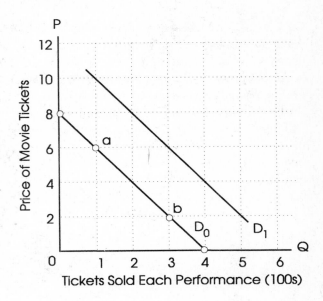

FIGURE 8

Another analytical technique used by economists is that of holding some variables constant when drawing a graph. The term ceteris paribus means to hold all other variables constant.

Curve D_0 in Figure 8 shows the relationship between the price of movie tickets and seat sold each performance. At $8 no one will purchase tickets, and if the movie is free (price = $0), 400 people will attend. Curve D_0 assumes a "typical" movie. Curve D_1 represents a change in this ceteris paribus assumption of a typical movie. Curve D_1, for example, might represent the demand for tickets when a movie starring Arnold Swartzenegger is showing.

When a curve shifts, check and see what ceteris paribus assumption has changed.

Graphs Without Numbers

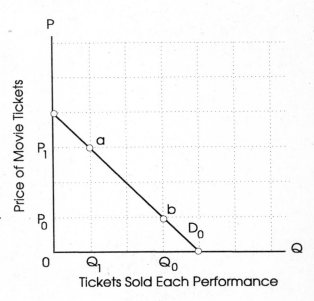

FIGURE 9

Graphs are often drawn without explicit numbers. While the exact value of an individual number is not known, how it relates to other numbers is often sufficient information to answer questions or solve a problem. Figure 9 duplicates D_0 from Figure 8, but only two points are identified. By looking at the location of the two points we can tell that $P_0 < P_1$ and that $Q_1 < Q_0$. We don't know the exact amount, but we do know that one point has a greater ticket price (P_1) and one point (Q_0) represents larger audiences.

Looking at Figure 8, we know that total sales (in dollars) at point a would be $6 per ticket times the number of tickets sold or $6 x 100 =

$600. In Figure 9, total sales would equal P_1 x Q_1 or be equal to area $0P_1aQ_1$. Areas are expressed by the points that enclose the area. Total sales at a price of $2 (point b) is also $600 ($2 x 300) or area $0P_0bQ_0$ in Figure 9.

Descriptive Graphs

Descriptive graphs are the most common figures in newspapers and magazines. They consist of bar, pie or line charts, and many others that may include line drawings or photos.

When reading a descriptive chart, first look at the title to get a basic idea of what is being presented. Then look close at the horizontal and vertical axes to determine what is being measured, paying particular attention to the units of measurement. Avoid looking at the chart values themselves until you know exactly what is on each axis. The meaning of the chart will often be much clearer if you follow this simple procedure.

Algebra

Simple Equation for a Straight Line

Straight or linear lines are typically used by economists to describe relationships between two variables. These lines can be described mathematically by a simple equation:

$$Y = a + bX$$

where X and Y are the independent and dependent variables respectively. Parameter a is the vertical intercept and parameter b is the slope of the line. Parameters do not change, they define the line. Note that this equation can be read as follows: To find any value of Y multiply X times b and add that value to a.

FIGURE 10

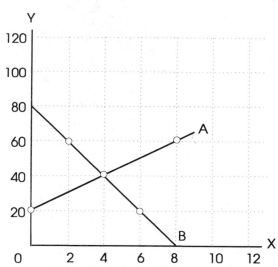

Figure 10 shows two lines A and B. Line A looks very much like the relationship described in Figure 1. The vertical intercept is equal to 20 and the slope is equal to 5. Therefore, the equation for line A is: $Y = 20 + 5X$. Substitute several values of X to see that this equation is correct.

Line B has a negative slope of -10. The vertical intercept is 80 and thus the equation for this line is:

$$Y = 80 - 10X.$$

Algebraic Manipulation of Equations

Consider the following simple equation:

$$A = \frac{B}{C}$$

Now assume that you had the values for A and C and needed to find the value for B. You would want to manipulate this equation so that B was on one side and the other variables were on the other side. To do that you would multiply both sides of the equation by C. Note that multiplying both sides of any equation by the same number does not change the fundamental relationship of the equation. Your resulting multiplication would yield:

$$C \times A = \frac{B \times C}{C}$$

Since the Cs on the right hand side cancel out, you are left with:

$$C \times A = B$$

Next, given the original equation, $A = B/C$, assume that you know A and B but want to find C. This is a little more complex, but involves the same general process. First, as before, we multiply both sides by C to get:

$$C \times A = B$$

Now divide both sides by A, and the result is:

$$\frac{C \times A}{A} = \frac{B}{A}$$

Since the As on the left hand side cancel out, we are left with:

$$C = \frac{B}{A}$$

This simple algebraic manipulation is used frequently to solve for various values of simple equations.

Solving Simple Sets of Equations

Consider the following two equations:

$$Y = 3X$$

$$X = 3 + 2Y$$

To solve for Y, we would substitute the right-hand side of the second equation into the first equation for the value of X, or;

$$Y = 3 \times (3 + 2Y)$$

$$Y = 9 + 6Y$$

Now, we have only one equation and one unknown. Thus,

$$Y - 6Y = 9$$

$$-5Y = 9$$

$$Y = 9/-5.$$

Now that we know the value of Y, we can plug this value into X equation ($X = 3 + 2Y$), yielding:

$$X = 3 + 2(-9/5)$$

$$X = 3 + -18/5$$

$$X = 15/5 + -18/5$$

$$X = -3/5.$$

Using this simple substitution technique, we are able to solve these two equations for consistent values of Y and X.

Computing Percentage Changes

Most of economic analysis deals with relative change in variables. Computing relative changes involves computing the percentage change from one position to the next. Computing percentage change involves the following:

$$\text{percentage change} = \frac{\text{current value} - \text{past value}}{\text{past value}} \times 100$$

For example, you expect your annual income to increase when you graduate from college, so let's assume that it rises from $10,000 to $25,000 after graduation. The percentage increase in your income is:

$$\frac{\$25,000 - \$10,000}{\$10,000} \times 100 = \frac{\$15,000}{\$10,000} \times 100 = 150\%$$

Now consider what happens if you get a 100% raise in your new salary the second year. A 100% raise will double your annual income to $50,000. Thus, you have received a 150% plus a 100% increase in annual income over two years. Has your total income increased by 250% (150% + 100%)? No! There is a compounding effect from the two raises. Your total annual income has increased from $10,000 to $50,000 for a total percentage increase of 400% (check this by using the above equation). This compounding effect, can, over a large number of years result in small interest payments compounding into large ending values.

Economic Analysis

Economic analysis involves the systematic description of a problem in such a way that specific conclusions can be reached. To make economic analysis simpler, do the follow:

- Examine the problem and decide which economic model can best be used to answer the questions posed. You will learn many economic models in this class and no one model can be used to answer all questions.
- Draw an initial graph that reflects the state of the world at the beginning of the problem.
- Take a moment to mentally review the assumptions inherent in the model. Often this review will help you proceed as you reexamine the description of the problem. Very often just reviewing the assumptions of the model will point you towards the solution.
- Proceed step-by-step. First, look to see what has been changed in the problem from the initial situation. Isolate that change and see where analysis of that change takes you. For most models and problems this means a change in the ceteris paribus assumptions. Economic models often hold a certain set of circumstances constant. Check to see if one of these factors previously held constant has changed. In economics, problems are generally staged from one change to the next.
- Make the changes in your graph and analyze the results.

Problems

Work through the following problems, then check your answers with the ones provided at the end of this section.

Matching

____ 1. dependent variable

____ 2. inverse relationship

____ 3. ceteris paribus

____ 4. scatter diagram

____ 5. slope

____ 6. independent variable

____ 7. 45° reference line

a. A graph that plots the values of one variable associated with another.

b. The rate at which the dependent variable grows for a given change in the independent variable.

c. A line where all values of the independent variable are equal to the dependent variable.

d. All other relevant variables stay the same.

e. Typically plotted on the horizontal axis.

f. Changes in this variable are the result of changes in another variable.

g. Changes in one variable move in the opposite direction to changes in the other variable

Essay Questions

1. Give an example of two variables that are directly related.

2. Give an example of two variables that are inversely related.

3. Describe how finding the slope of a curve differs from finding the slope of a straight line.

Graphs, Algebra, and Economic Analysis

Multiple Choice

_____ 1. Which of the following is most likely to be directly related to human happiness?
   a. war
   b. air pollution
   c. income
   d. pimples

_____ 2. Which of the following pairs of variables are most likely to be inversely related?
   a. Attendance at baseball games and number of people visiting Hawaii in January.
   b. Income and consumer spending.
   c. Annual inches of rain and number of species supported by the local environment.
   d. Infant mortality and access to prenatal health care.

_____ 3. Your friend Pentalope notices that the price of dog food has dropped from $12 to $9. By what percentage has the price of dog food dropped?
   a. 15%
   b. 20%
   c. 25%
   d. 33%

FIGURE 11

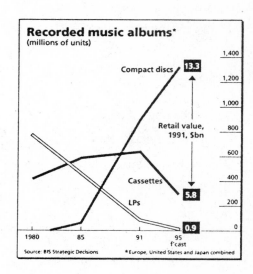

_____ 4. The sales of recorded music albums are shown in Figure 11 (Source: The Economist, 9-26-92, p. 119). Which of the following statements is true?
   a. Cassettes presently out sell compact disks.
   b. In 1992, the number of cassettes exceeded the number of LPs and compact disks combined.
   c. In 1985, the number of cassettes exceeded the number of LPs or compact disks.
   d. Total sales of cassettes and LPs exceeds that of compact discs.

Graphs, Algebra, and Economic Analysis

_____ 5. The cost of telephone calls to and from the United States from various countries is shown in Figure 12 (Source: The Economist, 9-12-92, p. 79). Which of the following statements is correct?
   a. It is cheaper to call the United States from Brazil than to call Brazil from the U.S.
   b. It costs 15 times more to call the U.S. from Spain than vice versa.
   c. In only one country is the cost of calling from abroad cheaper than calling from the U.S.
   d. The cost of calling between Japan and the U.S. is the same no matter which country you initiate the call.

FIGURE 12

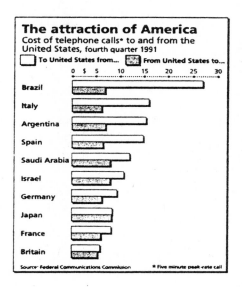

Problems

1. Use the data in Table 3 to answer the following questions.

TABLE 3

X	Y_1	Y_2
0	200	100
1	225	150
2	250	200
3	275	250
4	300	300
5	325	350
6	350	400
7	375	450
8	400	500
9	425	550

FIGURE 13

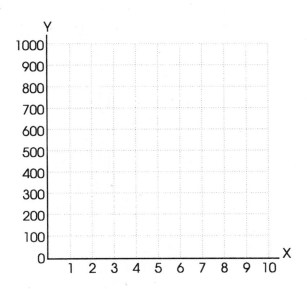

a. Plot lines Y_1 and Y_2 on Figure 13.

b. What is the slope of line Y_1?

c. What is the slope of line Y_2?

d. What is the equation for line Y_1?

e. What is the equation for line Y_2?

f. Between X=2 and X=6, which line has the largest percentage change in Y?

2. Figure 14 below shows the sales expectations of 16 countries covered in a recent survey by Dun and Bradstreet (Source: The Economist, 8-22-92, p. 87). Answer the questions that follow based on the data in this figure.

FIGURE 14

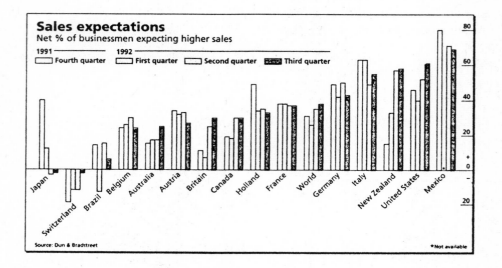

a. Which country consistently had the highest percent of its business people forecasting higher sales expectations?

b. What percent of the countries shown have a negative net percent of business people expecting sales increases in the most recent quarter surveyed?

c. Which country has the most pessimistic set of business people as reflected in this survey?

d. Which country had the greatest percentage increase in percent of its business people expecting higher sales between the 4th quarter of 1991 and 3rd quarter 1992?

Graphs, Algebra, and Economic Analysis

Answers to Problems

Matching

1. f
2. g
3. d
4. a
5. b
6. e
7. c

Essay

1. Examples would include: Body weight and calories, and income and education.
2. Examples would include: Number of pears purchased and the price per unit of pears, and speed and fuel consumption.
3. When you find the slope of a straight line, you compute the change in Y divided by the change in X or rise over run of the straight line. Finding the slope of a curve requires that you do the process describe above for a tangent to any point on the curve.

Multiple Choice

1. c
2. d
3. c
4. c
5. d

Problems

1a. See Figure 15.
1b. 25
1c. 50
1d. $Y_1 = 200 + 25X$
1e. $Y_2 = 100 + 50X$
1f. Y_2

2a. Mexico
2b. 2/16 = 12.5%
2c. Switzerland

FIGURE 15

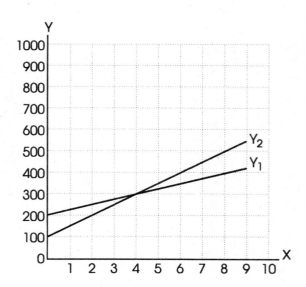

Graphs, Algebra, and Economic Analysis

HomeWork Set I-1
Introduction to Microeconomics
(Chapter 1)

Positive v. Normative Economics

Indicate whether the statement represents a positive or normative statement.

__1. The federal income tax should be proportional.
__2. Unemployment is caused by increases in the minimum wage.
__3. The purchase of American goods by the Japanese will result in low incomes in America.
__4. Adoption of cleaner production techniques by American companies will increase production costs and reduce output.

Opportunity Costs

This figure shows a hypothetical relationship between study time and grade point average for students with good, average, and poor study habits. Opportunity costs are defined as the value of the best alternative forgone when a choice is made. Assume for this example that we will measure opportunity costs in units of time. A student faces a choice on the use of time; study or leisure. Thus the opportunity cost of additional study time (and the resulting higher grade point average) is time lost for leisure activity.

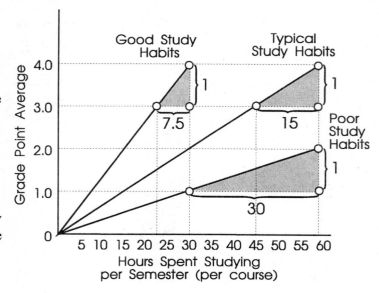

From the data provided in the graph, calculate the opportunity cost of increasing the grade point average by one full grade point for each type of student.

5. Opportunity cost for a student with good study habits (in hours)?
6. Opportunity cost for a student with typical or average study habits (in hours)?
7. Opportunity cost for a student with poor study habits (in hours)?

8. The poor student currently has a 2.0 GPA. How many hours per semester per course is the student studying?
9. How many additional hours per course, per semester would this student have to study to attain a 4.0 GPA?
10. How many additional hours of leisure would a good student enrolled in 5 classes gain if she allowed her GPA to fall from a 3.5 to 2.5?

Question for thought:

Assuming that the value of an hour of leisure is constant and is the same for all students and that the value of increasing the GPA by one grade point is also constant and the same for all students, why, besides poor study habits might the student with poor study habits be expected to have lower grades than the student with average or good study habits?

Tables and Graphs

Graphs and tables are now part of our everyday life. Computer-enhanced graphics have become a common element of local and national news broadcasts. Graphs provide visual representations of tabular data in an easy-to-understand format. Graphs report statistics, mathematical equations and relationships between variables. Charts and graphs are split into two categories, *descriptive* and *analytical*. While both types have many common elements, descriptive graphs typically report data and relationships based on actual data. Analytical figures, by contrast, are often hypothetical relationships, that permit us to logically derive conclusions once we agree upon the general shape and location of the curves.

Descriptive Graphs

Problem 1: Simple Descriptive Graphs

This figure provides a stylized picture of per capita Gross Domestic Product (GDP) for five selected countries as a percent of the average per capita GDP for all OECD (Organization for Economic Co-operation and Development) countries.

11. Which country had the highest GDP per capita in 1995?
12. Which country had the lowest growth rate of GDP per capita from 1970 to 1995?
13. Average OECD per capita GDP was $5,000 in 1970 and $20,000 in 1995. What has been the percentage change in Taiwan's per capita GDP since 1970?

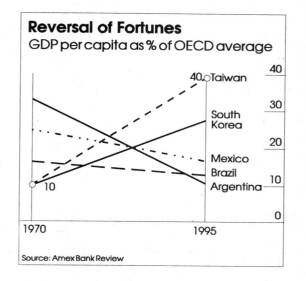

Problem 2: More Complex Descriptive Graphics

This figure shows the movements in the unemployment rate and the level of real GDP between 1928 and 1934.

14. What was the percentage change in real GDP between 1929 and 1933?
15. Does there appear to be a relationship between the change in real GDP and the unemployment rate? (yes/no)
16. What is the nature of the relationship? (direct/inverse/no relationship)

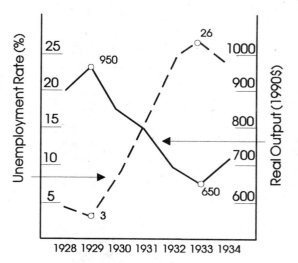

Analytical Graphs

An analytical graph shows precise relationships between specific economic variables. Descriptive figures plot economic data collected from required government reporting (income tax forms, birth and death certificates, etc.), surveys (Current Population Surveys, unemployment surveys, polls), or annual reports of various organizations. Analytical graphs posit a specific (often mathematical) relationship between variables.

Problem 3: Constructing A Graph & Computing Slope

This table provides data for a demand curve for a monopoly firm. The data are plotted in Panel A of the figure. The total revenue the firm can expect to receive from sales at any price can be calculated as $P \times Q = TR$. For each price and quantity given in the table (columns 1 and 2) calculate the expected total revenue and fill in column 3 of the table. Plot the total revenue curve in Panel B of the figure.

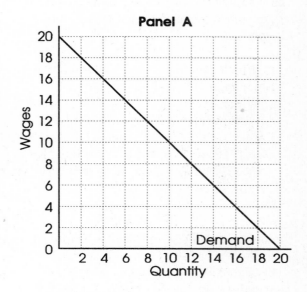

Price (P)	Quantity (Q)	Total Revenue (TR)
20	0	___
18	2	___
16	4	___
14	6	___
12	8	___
10	10	___
8	12	___
6	14	___
4	16	___
2	18	___
0	20	___

17. At what price and quantity does total revenue reach a maximum?
18. What is the slope of the total revenue curve at the level of output that maximizes total revenue?

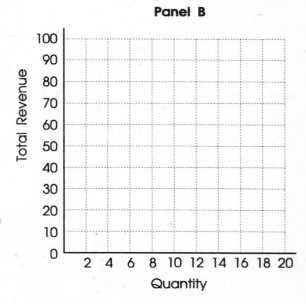

(For 19-21 estimate the slope of the total revenue curve by calculating the slope of a straight line connecting the given points)

19. What does the slope of the total revenue curve equal as output increases from 2 to 4 units?
20. What does the slope of the total revenue curve equal as output increase from 8 to 10 units?
21. What does the slope of the total revenue curve equal as output increases from 10 to 12 units?
22. What happens to the slope of the total revenue curve as output increases? (increase, decrease)

The slope of the total revenue curve ($\Delta TR/\Delta Q$) measures marginal revenue, an important economic concept that you will use later in the course. In panel A of the figure, plot the marginal revenue curve based on your answers to 19-21. For this graph treat the calculated slope as the marginal revenue of the mid-point of the two quantities given. Example: the approximate slope of the total revenue curve between an output of 2 and an output of 4 is ($64-$36)/2 = $14 . Plot $14 as the MR of the third unit.

23. At what level of output is marginal revenue equal to 0?
24. Where is the MR curve relative to the demand curve? (above, below)

Problem 4: Social Security -- Working With Percentage Changes

The annual cost-of-living increases for those drawing Social Security are listed in this table (six months were skipped in 1983 to help bail out the Social Security System).

25. How much (in percent) did Social Security payments increase from January 1984 to January 1992? (Hint: A percentage increase in one period is compounded in the next period. Simply adding up annual percentages will not capture this compounding.)

Month/ Year	Annual Increase (%)	Month/ Year	Annual Increase (%)
July 75	8.0	Jan 85	3.5
July 76	6.4	Jan 86	3.1
July 77	5.9	Jan 87	1.3
July 78	6.5	Jan 88	4.2
July 79	9.9	Jan 89	4.0
July 80	14.3	Jan 90	4.7
July 81	11.2	Jan 91	5.4
July 82	7.4	Jan 92	3.7
Jan 84	3.5		

Answers HomeWork I-1

(a)	yes	(a)	-31.6	(a)	positive	(a)	above
(b)	no	(b)	32	(b)	normative	(b)	below
(c)	7.5	(c)	Argentina	(c)	$10, 10 units	(c)	undefined or infinite
(d)	15	(d)	10	(d)	14	(d)	38.7
(e)	30	(e)	Mexico	(e)	2	(e)	-28
(a)	60	(a)	South Korea	(a)	inverse	(a)	16.6
(b)	37.5	(b)	Taiwan	(b)	direct	(b)	.50
(c)	100	(c)	increase	(c)	no relationship	(c)	12.4
(d)	150	(d)	decrease	(d)	-2	(d)	25.7
(e)	1500	(e)	28	(e)	0	(e)	45

HomeWork Set I-2
Production Possibilities Analysis
(Chapter 2)

Basic Production Possibilities Analysis

The Production Possibilities model describes the limits of what a society can produce. Consider the following production possibilities, then plot, label and connect the points to form a Production Possibilities Frontier (PPF) in the figure.

Production Possibility	Mangoes	Passion Fruit
A	500	0
B	400	200
C	300	350
D	200	425
E	100	475
F	0	500

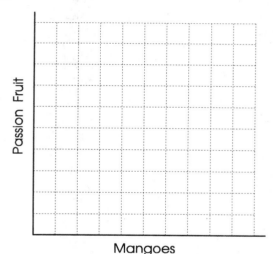

List the three main assumptions of the PPF model.
    a.
    b.
    c.

1. What shape does the PPF have? (linear, concave, convex)
2. What does the shape of the PPF suggest about the opportunity cost of producing additional mangoes or   passion fruit? (increases, decreases, constant)

Draw point (300, 300) on your graph. Label the point G.

3. What can you say about this level of output? (obtainable, unobtainable)
4. What can you say about the use of resources? (unobtainable, efficient, inefficient)

Opportunity Cost and Production Possibility Analysis

Using the PPF you graphed in the figure above, what is the opportunity cost for passion fruit (in terms of mangoes per passion fruit) for each of the following moves:

Move
5. 0 to 200?
6. 200 to 350?
7. 350 to 425?
8. 425 to 475?
9. 475 to 500?

Intermediate Production Possibilities Analysis

Answer the following True/False questions based on this figure.

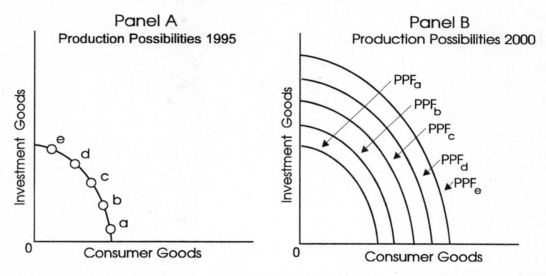

___10. If present consumption were higher than the level of consumption at point a, the future PPF would lie inside PPF$_a$.

___11. PPF$_e$ could be reached by the year 2000 if the current investment-consumption choice is point c.

___12. Successful government policies to increase current savings could move the 1995 economy from a point like b to a point like c.

___13. The more successful a savings policy, the lower the future expected growth.

___14. Shifting more resources to the production of capital goods in 1996 causes the 1995 PPF to shift outward.

___15. The figure implies that the opportunity cost of higher future growth is less current consumption.

Comparative Advantage and Production Possibilities

Consider the following Production Possibilities Frontiers for the United States and China. Presently both countries are producing and consuming both goods as shown by points a in the figure.

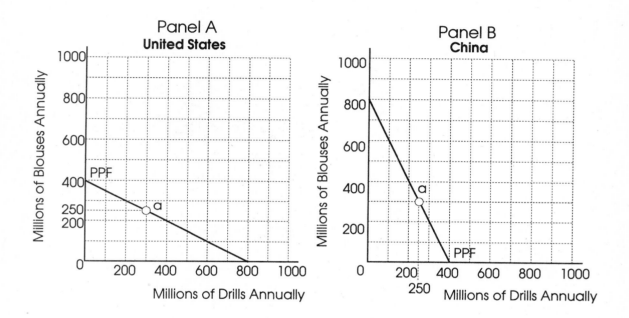

Define comparative advantage:

16. What is the cost of a drill in terms of blouses per drill in the US?
17. Which country has a comparative advantage in drills?
18. Which country is the least cost (opportunity cost) producer of blouses?

Assume each country specializes and produces only the product for which it has a comparative advantage.

19. Which country would produce drills? How many?
20. Which country would produce blouses? How many?

Draw the Consumption Possibilities Frontier (CPF) for each country after trade commences--
assume that each country specializes in the product they produce most efficiently (lowest
opportunity cost), and that the trading ratio is 1:1. Label the curves CPF. Further assume that
trade occurs in such a way that each country consumes equal amounts of each good. Label the
point where each country will be on its CPF as point b.

21. Are both countries better off? (yes, no)
22. What is the quantity of exports from the US to China?
23. What is the quantity of exports from China?
24. What is the gain to China from trade?
25. What is the gain to the US from trade?

Answers for HomeWork I-2

(a) linear	(a) efficient	(a) United States
(b) concave	(b) inefficient	(b) China
(c) convex	(c) .5	(c) US, 800
(d) increases	(d) .67	(d) China, 800
(e) decreases	(e) 1.33	(e) China, 400

(a) constant	(a) 2	(a) US, 300
(b) obtainable	(b) 4	(b) 400 drills
(c) unobtainable	(c) 1.67	(c) 400 blouses
(d) no	(d) true	(d) 150 drills, 100 blouses
(e) yes	(e) false	(e) 100 drills, 150 blouses

HomeWork Set I-3
Supply and Demand Analysis
(Chapters 3 & 4)

Determinants Of Supply and Demand

Which of the factors affecting demand or supply is most relevant when:

1. the demand for skiing in Colorado increases due to a National Weather Service report predicting record snowfall for the upcoming winter season?
2. an increase in lift ticket prices leads to a reduction in the demand for skiing equipment?
3. the demand for oat bran rises due to reports that it helps reduce cholesterol?
4. the demand for many goods and services increases this year when Congress announces a new national sales tax to begin next year?
5. the supply of personal computers increases due to a decrease in the price of memory chips?
6. a hurricane in Florida results in a decrease in the supply of citrus fruit?

Simple Market Equilibrium Analysis

Use this figure to answer the following questions.

7. The equilibrium market price is?
8. Quantity demanded at a price of $30 is?
9. Quantity supplied at a price of $30 is?
10. A surplus of how much occurs at a price of $30?

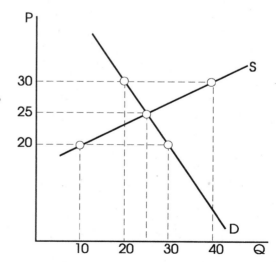

More Complex Market Analysis

Use this figure to answer the following questions concerning three different product markets. questions For each product assume that the market begins in equilibrium at the intersection of D_0 and S_0 (point e). What is the new equilibrium point in:

The market for compact discs (**CDs**), when:

11. the price of CD players decreases?
12. the economy suffers high unemployment?
13. an energy tax raises the cost of the plastic used to manufacture CDs?

The market for **Spam** (inferior good), when:

14. there is a cut in income taxes?
15. the tonight show holds a multimillion dollar Spam sculpting contest?
16. the price of pig feed increases (Spam is a pork product) at the same time that Spam is reported to raise cholesterol levels?
17. the price of bologna (a substitute) decreases at the same time there is a surge in the pig population.

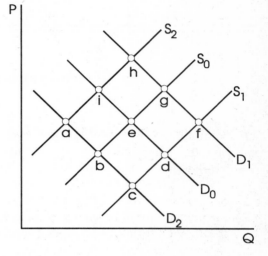

The market for **four-wheel drive vehicles**, when:

18. import tariffs on these vehicles are reduced while the real price of gasoline decreases?
19. population growth rates in mountainous and snowy regions rise well above the national average.
20. government regulations require vehicle manufacturers to make costly adjustments in order to improve fuel efficiency and reduce auto emissions.

Price Controls: Minimum Wage

Use the information in this table concerning the market for unskilled labor to answer the following questions.

21. A minimum wage of $6 per hour would result in total unemployment of ___ million workers.

22. ___ million unemployed new workers enter the labor force due to a $6 per hour minimum wage.

23. A minimum wage of $3 per hour would result in total unemployment of ___ million workers.

Hourly Wage Rate	Quantity of Labor Supplied (millions)	Quantity of Labor Demanded (millions)
2.00	10	50
3.00	20	40
4.00	30	30
5.00	40	20
6.00	50	10
7.00	60	0
8.00	70	0
9.00	80	0

Price Controls: Rent Control

Use the information in this table concerning the market for two bedroom apartments to answer the following questions.

24. A rent ceiling of $500 per month would result in a shortage of ___ thousand apartments.

25. A rent ceiling of $600 per month would result in a shortage of ___ thousand apartments.

Monthly Rent	Quantity Supplied (1,000s)	Quantity Demanded (1,000s)
400	5	35
450	10	30
500	15	25
550	20	20
600	25	15
650	30	10
700	35	5
750	40	0

Answers for HomeWork I-3

(a)	-20
(b)	-10
(c)	0
(d)	10
(e)	15

(a)	point a
(b)	point b
(c)	point c
(d)	point d
(e)	point e

(a)	Tastes and preferences
(b)	Income and its distribution
(c)	Prices of related goods
(d)	Number and ages of buyers
(e)	The good's own price

(a)	20
(b)	25
(c)	30
(d)	35
(e)	40

(a)	point f
(b)	point g
(c)	point h
(d)	point i
(e)	point j

(a)	Technology
(b)	Resource costs
(c)	Prices of other producible goods
(d)	Expectations
(e)	Number of sellers

HomeWork Set I-4
Elasticity and Consumer Choice
(Chapters 5 & 6)

Price Elasticity Of Demand And Other Elasticities

Suppose that when the price per case of Bullmoose, a locally brewed beer, falls from $16 to $14, the quantity demanded rises from 200 to 300 cases per week.

1. What is the price elasticity of demand (absolute value) for Bullmoose beer?
2. What will happen to Bullmoose Brewery's total revenue in response to this price change? (increase, decrease)
3. What would happen to the price elasticity of demand for Bullmoose if two more breweries were established in the community? (increase, decrease)

Wile E. Coyote has an annual income of $20,000 and attends 3 Grateful Dead concerts per year. After Wile E. wins the lottery (an easier task than catching the roadrunner), his income increases to $40,000 annually, and he attends 5 Dead concerts per year.

4. What is Wile E. Coyote's income elasticity of demand for Grateful Dead concerts?
5. Given your previous answer, what type of good are Grateful Dead concerts for Wile E.? (normal, inferior)

Currently 100 tennis racquets ($50 each) and 80 sets of golf clubs ($200 a set) are sold in Sportsville each month.

6. What is the cross price elasticity of demand for tennis racquets when a $100 increase in the price of golf clubs increases the sale of tennis racquets to 150 per month?

Elasticity And Tax Incidence

This figure illustrates a tax in the market for gasoline. Use this information to answer the following questions.

7. What is the amount of the tax, in cents per gallon, depicted in this diagram?
8. What percentage of this tax falls on consumers?
9. What would happen to the percentage of the tax that producers pay if demand were to become more elastic? (increase, decrease)

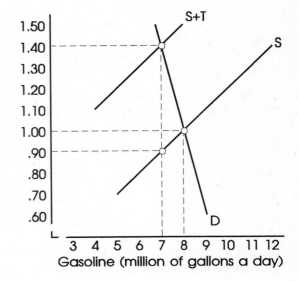

Who would bear the economic incidence of a tax (producers only, consumers only, producers and consumers equally, producers and consumers but unequally) levied in the market illustrated by:

10. Panel a?
11. Panel b?
12. Panel c?
13. Panel d?

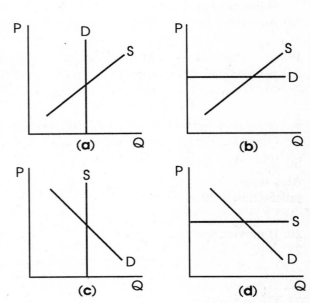

Marginal Utility Analysis

Complete this table, showing Guido's utility from beer and pizza, to answer the following questions.

Glasses of Beer	Total Utility (Beer)	Marginal Utility (Beer)	$P_b = \$2$ MU/P_b	$P_b = \$1$ MU/P_b	Slices of Pizza	Total Utility (Pizza)	Marginal Utility (Pizza)	$P_p = \$2$ MU/P_p
0	0	xxx	xxx	xxx	0	0	xxx	xxx
1	25				1	20		
2	45				2	35		
3	60				3	45		
4	65				4	50		
5	69				5	52		
6	70				6	52		

14. What is Guido's marginal utility from consuming the fifth beer?
15. What is Guido's total utility from consuming four slices of pizza?
16. Suppose that Guido has $10 to spend, that both goods cost $2 each, and that Guido is a utility maximizer. How many slices of pizza will he purchase (assume he spends the whole $10)?
17. Now suppose that the price of beer drops to $1 per glass. How many slices of pizza will Guido now purchase if his $10 budget is unchanged?
18. According to your answers to the previous two questions, what is the sign (positive or negative) of the cross price elasticity of demand between beer and pizza?
19. Guido receives some money from his aunt and now has $16 to spend. If beer still costs $1 per glass and pizza $2 per slice, how many beers will Guido buy to maximize his utility?

Consumer Equilibrium

Suppose that Muffy spends all of her income on two goods, movie rentals and paperback novels. Also suppose that she chooses a particular bundle of these two goods such that the incremental satisfaction is 20 utils from the last movie, and 30 utils from the last novel.

20. If movies rent for $2 and the price of novels is $3, is Muffy maximizing her total utility?
21. Muffy's total utility will be maximized by purchasing (*more*, *less*, her *present* quantity of) movies and (*more*, *less*, her *present* quantity of) novels.
22. If both goods cost $2, is Muffy maximizing her total utility?
23. Given the prices in the previous question, Muffy's total utility will be maximized by purchasing (*more*, *less*, her *present* quantity of) movies and (*more*, *less*, her *present* quantity of) novels.

Consumer Surplus

This figure shows Dapper Dan's demand for the new "miracle" hair growth formula, Hirsute, which currently sells for a uniform price of $70 a liter.

24. The consumer surplus Dan derives from the second liter of Hirsute equals $?
25. Dan's total consumer surplus from purchasing Hirsute equals $? (Assume that Hirsute can be purchased in infinitesimally small units)

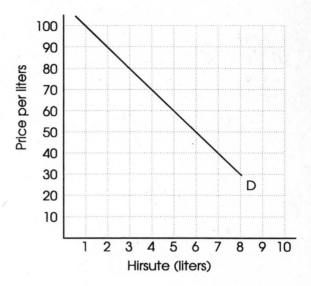

Answers for HomeWork I-4

(a) -1/3	(a) more, more	(a) decrease	(a) 1.0
(b) 4/3	(b) less, more	(b) normal	(b) 2.0
(c) 5/3	(c) more, less	(c) complement	(c) 2.8
(d) -1.0	(d) present, less	(d) substitute	(d) 3.0
(e) 20	(e) more, present	(e) increase	(e) 3.6

(a) 50	(a) present, present	(a) inferior	(a) 4.0
(b) 160	(b) producers only	(b) positive	(b) 5.0
(c) 80	(c) producers & consumers but unequally	(c) negative	(c) 6.0
(d) 90	(d) producers & consumers equally	(d) no	(d) 69.0
(e) 120	(e) consumers only	(e) yes	(e) 0.75

HomeWork Set I-5
Production and Costs
(Chapter 8)

Short Run Production and Costs

The production management team at Speedy's Microwave Burritos needs your help ascertaining the productivity and associated costs of hiring various levels of employees. To accomplish this task, you will need to complete the columns for average product of labor (APP_L), marginal product of labor (MPP_L), average variable cost (AVC), and marginal cost (MC) in the table below (round all numbers to 2 decimal places). Output is measured in cases per week, and each employee is paid $400 per week (the firm's only variable cost).

Labor	Output	APP_L	MPP_L	AVC	MC
0	0	xxx	xxx	xxx	xxx
1	8				
2	18				
3	32				
4	52				
5	68				
6	76				
7	80				
8	82				

1. What is the average physical product of four workers?
2. What is the marginal physical product of the sixth worker?
3. What is the average variable cost of producing 80 cases of burritos per week?
4. What is the marginal cost of increasing production from 52 to 68 cases a week?
5. What is the additional amount of output gained by hiring the fourth worker?
6. What happens to average variable costs and marginal costs as output is expanded? (rise then fall, fall then rise)

Short Run Costs

This table provides the hourly production schedule at Fuzz Bumpers, Inc., a bumper sticker manufacturer. Plant and overhead costs are $100, and the wage is $15. Complete the table, rounding all numbers to 2 decimal places.

Labor	Output	TVC	TC	AFC	AVC	ATC	MC
0	0			xxx	xxx	xxx	xxx
1	60						
2	150						
3	260						
4	380						
5	490						
6	570						
7	610						
8	630						
9	635						

7. What is the total cost (in dollars) of producing 630 bumper stickers?
8. What is the additional cost (in cents per sticker) of raising output from 380 to 490 stickers?
9. When producing 490 stickers, what is the variable cost per sticker (in cents)?
10. What is the total variable cost (in dollars) of producing 150 bumper stickers?
11. What does each bumper sticker cost to make (in cents) if 610 are produced?
12. At an output level of 380 stickers, what is average fixed cost (in cents)?

Relationship Between Production and Costs

Use this figure, which shows cost information for Lenny's Lobsters, Inc. to answer the following questions.

13. What is the total variable cost (in thousands of dollars) of producing 50,000 lobsters?
14. What is the amount of Lenny's total fixed cost (in thousands of dollars)?
15. What is Lenny's fixed cost per lobster (in dollars) at an output level of 60,000?
16. At an output level of 70,000, what do total costs equal (in thousands of dollars)?

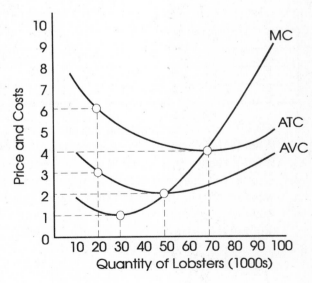

17. Do these cost curves represent the short run or the long run?
18. Is the law of diminishing marginal returns a short run or long run phenomenon?
19. At what level of output (in thousands) does Lenny's production of lobsters begin to experience diminishing marginal returns?
20. At what level of output (in thousands) does the average physical product of labor (APP$_L$) at Lenny's Lobsters, Inc. begin to fall?

Long Run Costs

As the forward looking CEO of Busy Bee Candles, Inc. you realize that your current plant is too small for the volume of production your company has achieved. You therefore decide to build a new and bigger plant. Potential plant sizes A, B, and C, (all of which are larger than Busy Bee's current plant), and their associated monthly short run average cost curves are shown in the figure.

21. In the range of output experiencing economies of scale, what happens to your costs per unit as output is expanded? (rise, fall)
22. Which plant size would you choose if you expect to be producing 8 million candles per month?
23. Which plant size would you choose if you expected to be producing 5 million candles per month?
24. Which plant is **not** the least-cost plant for producing 4 million candles per month?
25. Long run average costs are minimized at what level of output (in millions)?

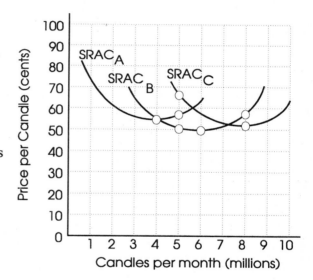

Answers for HomeWork I-5

(a) 1
(b) 2
(c) 3
(d) 4
(e) 5

(a) plant A
(b) plant B
(c) plant C
(d) plants A or B
(e) plants B or C

(a) rise
(b) fall
(c) 220
(d) rise then fall
(e) fall then rise

(a) 11
(b) 12
(c) 13
(d) 14
(e) 15

(a) 6
(b) 7
(c) 8
(d) 9
(e) 100

(a) plants A or C
(b) plants A, B, or C
(c) 26
(d) 50
(e) can't tell

(a) 34
(b) long run
(c) 280
(d) short run
(e) nothing

(a) 20
(b) 25
(c) 30
(d) 35
(e) 60

HomeWork Set I-6
The Competitive Ideal
(Chapter 9)

Short Run Profit Maximization

In order to earn money for college expenses, you decide to open a pizza joint called PizzaDeals. Total cost information for your single product, large extra-cheese pizzas, is provided in this table. The market for pizza in your town is extremely competitive, and the market price of large extra-cheese pizzas is $7. Complete the table, and answer the following questions.

Output	TC	ATC	AFC	AVC	MC	MR
0	$10	xxx	xxx	xxx	xxx	xxx
1	14					
2	17					
3	19					
4	22					
5	26					
6	31					
7	37					
8	44					
9	52					

1. What is the amount of total fixed costs?

2. What is the marginal revenue from the fourth pizza?

3. What is AFC if you produce five pizzas?

4. What is AVC if you produce six pizzas?

5. If you make 8 pizzas, what does each one cost you to produce on average?

6. What is the marginal cost of producing the seventh pizza?

7. Assuming that you want to maximize profit, how many pizzas should you make?
8. What is the amount of economic profit (or loss) *per pizza* that you experience if you produce at the profit-maximizing level?

As Tren Dee Apparel's chief executive officer, you decide to break into the competitive sweatshirt market. Use the information provided in this figure to answer the following questions concerning Tren Dee's operations.

9. What is the equilibrium market price of sweatshirts?

10. What is the profit-maximizing level of output for Tren Dee (in thousands)?

11. At the profit-maximizing level of output, what is Tren Dee's total revenue (in thousands of dollars)?

12. What is Tren Dee's total cost (in thousands of dollars) at the profit-maximizing level of output?

13. At the profit-maximizing level of output, are economic profits positive, negative, or zero?

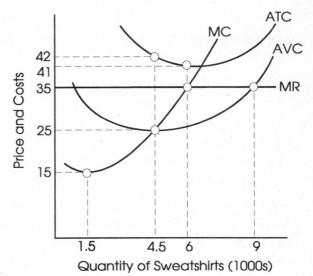

14. You should shutdown Tren Dee's sweatshirt operation if the market price falls below what dollar amount?

Firm And Industry Supply Curves

Cost information for Ledbetter, a typical *firm* in the competitive pencil industry, is provided in this table.

15. How many cases of pencils would Ledbetter supply if the market price were $6?

16. What quantity would Ledbetter supply if the market price were $3?

17. What quantity would Ledbetter supply if the market price were $1?

Output (Cases)	ATC	AFC	AVC	MC
0	xxx	xxx	xxx	xxx
1	$8.00	$5.00	$3.00	$3.00
2	5.00	2.50	2.50	2.00
3	3.67	1.67	2.00	1.00
4	3.25	1.25	2.00	2.00
5	3.20	1.00	2.20	3.00
6	3.33	0.83	2.50	4.00
7	3.57	0.71	2.86	5.00
8	3.88	0.63	3.25	6.00
9	4.22	0.56	3.67	7.00

Suppose that there are 100 identical firms in the pencil industry (including Ledbetter). Complete the table at the right by determining total quantity supplied at the various prices.

18. What is total quantity supplied at a market price of $7?

19. What is the short run equilibrium price in this market?

Price ($)	Quantity Demanded (Cases)	Quantity Supplied (Cases)
1	900	
2	850	
3	800	
4	750	
5	700	
6	650	
7	600	

Long Run Adjustments

Use this figure, which illustrates short run cost and revenue conditions for a typical firm in the competitive laser printer industry, to answer the following questions.

20. The short run market price is?

21. In the long run, what will happen to the number of firms in the industry? (increase, decrease, remain the same)

22. In the long run, what will happen to the market supply curve for laser printers? (shift right, shift left, remain the same)

23. In the long run, what will happen to market price? (increase, decrease, remain the same)

24. In the long run, what will happen to economic profits (or losses) in this industry? (increase, decrease, remain the same)

25. Assuming this is a constant cost industry, the long run equilibrium price will be?

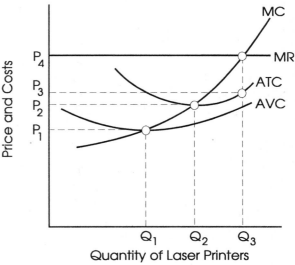

Answers for HomeWork Set I-6

(a) 1.50
(b) 2.00
(c) 2.50
(d) 3.50
(e) 5.00

(a) 10
(b) 20
(c) 25
(d) 30
(e) 35

(a) P_1
(b) P_2
(c) P_3
(d) P_4
(e) Q_1

(a) increase
(b) decrease
(c) remain the same
(d) shift right
(e) shift left

(a) 5.50
(b) 6.00
(c) 7.00
(d) 8.00
(e) 9.00

(a) 41
(b) 210
(c) 246
(d) 700
(e) 900

(a) Q_2
(b) Q_3
(c) positive
(d) negative
(e) zero

HomeWork Set I-7
Monopoly
(Chapter 10)

Barriers To Entry

Determine which of the three basic types of barriers to entry (natural, regulatory, or strategic) each of the following examples represent:

1. There is only one electric company serving a metropolitan area.
2. You cannot produce and sell your latest invention because it has already been patented.
3. The only restaurants you see on a publically operated toll road in Illinois are Hardees fast food restaurants.
4. A company spends an enormous amount of money to make its product a household name.
5. You have many choices for long distance phone service, but you only have one choice for local phone service.
6. The Organization of Petroleum Exporting Countries (OPEC) prices oil so that outsiders cannot easily compete.

Monopoly Profit Maximization

The table below provides partial information for Putrid Gas & Electric, a monopoly operating in the northwestern United States. The executives at Putrid would not divulge any more information than given in this table, so it is up to you to fill in the holes. Complete the table and use it to answer the questions that follow. (The output is electricity in thousands of kilowatt hours.)

Output	Price	TR	MR	TC	ATC	MC	Profit
0	xxx		xxx	110	xxx	xxx	
1			90		$144		
2						29	-3
3	80						42
4		300			56.75		
5				261			89
6			40	301			
7	60			348.5			
8	55					55	
9		450					-23.5
10			0			90	

7. What is total revenue (in dollars) if Putrid Gas and Electric produces two thousand kilowatt hours (KWHs) of electricity?
8. What is the marginal revenue (in dollars) of the four thousandth KWH?
9. How much does it cost Putrid (in total dollars) to produce two thousand KWHs?
10. What is the cost per unit (in dollars) of producing three thousand KWHs?
11. What is the marginal cost to Putrid (in dollars) of producing the nine thousandth KWH?
12. If Putrid Gas and Electric produces four thousand KWHs, what is its profit (in dollars)?
13. Using the MR = MC rule, what is the profit-maximizing level of output (in thousands of KWHs)?
14. What price will Putrid charge (in dollars) for the profit-maximizing level of output?

Welfare Loss Due To Monopoly

Suppose that tire sales in your town are controlled by Burn-Rubber Tires (BRT), a monopoly firm whose cost and revenue structure are shown in this figure.

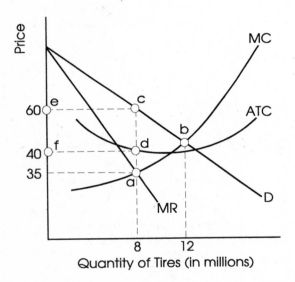

15. What price (in dollars) will BRT charge for its tires in order to maximize profit?
16. What is the profit-maximizing level of output for BRT (in millions)?
17. What is the amount of profit or loss (in millions of dollars) that BRT earns?
18. What, approximately, is the welfare loss (in millions of dollars) that results from BRT being the sole provider of tires?

Price Discrimination

Captain Video is a firm that sells used videos to three different groups: college students, senior citizens, and yuppies. Demand schedules for each of these groups are given in the tables below. Complete these tables and use the information to answer the following questions. Marginal cost equals $14 and is constant at all levels of output.

College Students				Senior Citizens				Yuppies			
Q	P	TR	MR	Q	P	TR	MR	Q	P	TR	MR
0	$28	$0	xxx	0	$19	$0	xxx	0	$35	$0	xxx
1	26			1	18			1	32		
2	24			2	17			2	29		
3	22			3	16			3	26		
4	20			4	15			4	23		
5	18			5	14			5	20		
6	16			6	13			6	17		
7	14			7	12			7	14		
8	12			8	11			8	12		
9	10			9	10			9	9		

Assuming that the firm maximizes profit, and that the conditions are right to price discriminate, what price (in dollars) would be charged to:

19. college students?
20. senior citizens?
21. yuppies?

What is the profit maximizing quantity that will be sold to:

22. College Students?
23. Senior citizens?
24. Yuppies?
25. Which of the following is one of the three requirements that must be met for a monopolist to be able to price discriminate? (Market must be competitive, Buyers must have the ability to resell the product, The firm must have market power, Demand must be elastic)

Answers for HomeWork Set I-7

(a) Market must be competitive
(b) Buyers must have ability to resell the product
(c) Not a barrier
(d) Economies of Scale must exist
(e) Natural barrier

(a) 14
(b) 16
(c) 20
(d) 23
(e) 50

(a) 0
(b) 1
(c) 2
(d) 3
(e) 4

(a) 100
(b) 144
(c) 160
(d) 166
(e) 170

(a) Strategic barrier
(b) The Firm must have market power
(c) Demand must be elastic
(d) Regulatory barrier
(e) Demand must be inelastic

(a) 60
(b) 65
(c) 66
(d) 70
(e) 73

(a) 5
(b) 6
(c) 7
(d) 8
(e) 9

(a) 173
(b) 240
(c) 280
(d) 320
(e) 480

HomeWork Set I-8
Monopolistic Competition, Oligopoly, and Strategic Behavior
(Chapters 11 & 12)

Monopolistic Competition In The Short Run

Demand and cost information for Old West Jeans, a producer in the monopolistically competitive blue jeans industry, is given in this table. Complete the table and answer the following questions.

Price	Output (1000s)	TR	MR	TC ($1000s)	ATC	MC
$100	0		xxx	$110	xxx	xxx
90	1			128		
80	2			150		
70	3			176		
60	4			206		
50	5			240		
40	6			278		
30	7			320		
20	8			366		
10	9			416		

1. What is the amount of sales revenue (in thousands of dollars) Old West would receive if it produced and sold 9 thousand pairs of jeans?
2. What is the additional revenue (in dollars) that Old West would gain by producing the 3 thousandth pair of jeans?
3. What is the additional cost (in dollars) to Old West of producing the 4 thousandth pair of jeans?
4. If Old West produced and sold 5 thousand pairs of jeans, what would be its profit per pair (in dollars)?
5. Up to how many thousands of pairs of jeans should Old West produce if it wants to maximize profits?
6. What price (in dollars) should Old West charge for its jeans (assuming that it produces the profit-maximizing quantity)?

7. How much profit (in thousands of dollars) does Old West earn at its profit maximizing output?
8. Is this situation (producing at the profit maximizing level of output) a possible long run equilibrium for Old West Jeans? (yes, no)

Monopolistic Competition In The Long Run

Use this figure, which illustrates cost and revenue data for Spike! (a typical firm in the monopolistically competitive soft drink industry), to answer the following questions.

9. What price (in cents) will Spike! charge for its product?
10. What quantity (in millions) will Spike! produce?
11. Economic profit for Spike! equals?
12. If Spike! were a competitive firm, what quantity (in millions) would it produce?
13. What is the amount of excess capacity (in millions of 12oz cans) for Spike!?

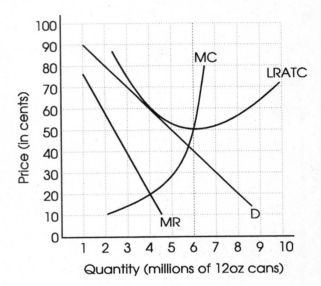

Concentration Ratios

Suppose that sales (in millions of dollars) by firms in the computer industry are as follows: Applepie=$190, BOB=$80, CSNY=$90, Dealtyme=$165, EFX=$62, Family=$220, Georgia=$130, Hummer=$255, Iditacomp=$75, Jynx=$115. Assume that these are the only firms in this industry.

14. What is the four-firm concentration ratio (in percentage terms) for this industry?
15. What is the eight-firm concentration ratio (in percentage terms) for this industry?

Oligopoly And Joint Profit Maximization

Deodorant producing firms around the world have joined together to form a cartel, commonly known as SWEAT, in an attempt to reap monopoly profits. This figure illustrates the cost and revenue data for the cartel and for one of the eight identical firms in the cartel.

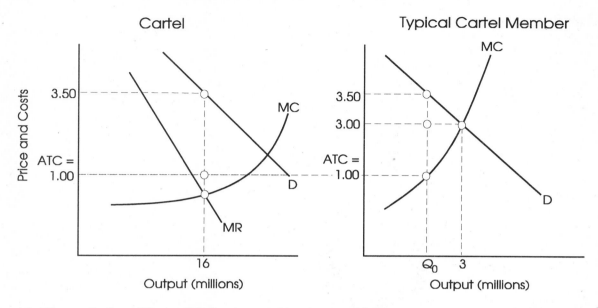

16. The profit (in millions of dollars) earned by the cartel is?
17. What is each members' share (in millions of dollars) of the cartel's profit?
18. Each cartel member has agreed to restrict output (in millions) to?
19. What is the approximate amount (in millions of dollars) of **additional** profit a cartel member can earn by cheating?

Game Theory

Suppose that the governments of two countries, Oz and Lilliput, are each deciding whether or not to impose tariffs on all imported commodities from the other country. Both governments want to choose the strategy that will benefit its country the most. The payoffs to each country (Oz,Lilliput) for each combination of strategies (tariffs, no tariffs) are given below. Use this information to answer the following questions.

20. What is the dominant strategy for Oz?
21. What is the dominant strategy for Lilliput?
22. What is the Nash equilibrium?

		Lilliput	
		Tariffs	No Tariffs
Oz	Tariffs	40, 40	170, 80
	No Tariffs	30, 100	150, 140

A duopoly industry (two firms) with no collusion consists of firms A and B which are essentially identical. Each firm can choose either a high advertising budget, or a low advertising budget. If both firms choose a high budget, then each firm will experience economic profits of zero (a normal rate of return). If both firms choose a low advertising budget, then each will reap positive economic profits equal to 5. If one firm chooses a high budget while the other pursues a low budget, then the high budget firm will enjoy economic profits of 12 and the low budget firm will realize negative profits equal to -5. Using this information, fill in the payoff matrix in the table, and answer the following questions. (High corresponds to a high advertising budget, and Low corresponds to a low advertising budget.)

23. What is the dominant strategy for firm A?
24. What is the dominant strategy for firm B?
25. What is the Nash equilibrium in this game?

Firm B

		High	Low
Firm A	High		
	Low		

Answers for HomeWork Set I-8

(a) 0 (a) 20 (a) Yes (a) Both countries choose tariffs
(b) 1 (b) 30 (b) No (b) Both countries choose no tariffs
(c) 2 (c) 34 (c) High (c) Oz--tariffs, Lilliput--no tariffs
(d) 3 (d) 40 (d) Low (d) Oz--no tariffs, Lilliput--tarrifs
(e) 4 (e) 50 (e) Tariffs (e) Need more information

(a) 5 (a) 60 (a) No tariffs (a) Both firms choose high
(b) 6 (b) 70 (b) No dominant strategy (b) Both firms choose low
(c) 7 (c) 80 (c) Price equals ATC (c) Firm A--low, Firm B--high
(d) 8 (d) 90 (d) Price equals MC (d) Firm A--high, Firm B--low
(e) 9 (e) 100 (e) MR = MC (e) Price does not equal ATC

HomeWork Set I-9
Factor Markets and Capitalization
(Chapters 13 - 15)

A Competitive Firm's Demand For Labor

You own a sandwich shop that excels at providing quality sandwiches for hungry lunch-time customers for just $2 each. The prevailing market wage rate (for labor) is $8 per hour. Complete this table and answer the following questions.

1. What is the marginal revenue product (in dollars) of the sixth unit of labor?
2. What is the marginal factor cost (in dollars) of labor for your sandwich shop?
3. What is your total labor cost per hour (in dollars) at an output level of 34 sandwiches?
4. What is the profit-maximizing amount of labor to hire?
5. If the cost of materials (breads, meats, cheeses, etc.) is $0.465 per sandwich, and materials costs are the only costs other than labor, then what is your total profit (in rounded dollars) at the profit-maximizing level of output?

Labor	Output	MPP$_L$	MRP	MFC
0	0	xxx	xxx	xxx
1	6			
2	13			
3	21			
4	28			
5	34			
6	39			
7	43			
8	46			
9	48			

Shifts In The Competitive Demand For Labor

A competitive firm in Mexico hires workers to produce colorful blankets woven from cotton. For each of the following scenarios, determine whether there will be an *increase, decrease,* or *no change* in the competitive firm's demand for labor.

6. Insects destroy a significant amount of the world cotton crop, leading to an increase in the price of cotton.
7. The amount of tourists traveling to Mexico quadruples.
8. Old weaving machines are replaced with newer, more efficient machines.

9. A trade agreement with the U.S. leads to an increased demand for Mexican products.
10. The equilibrium market price of Mexican blankets falls.

Elasticity Of Demand For Labor

Suppose that a competitive food processing company uses labor, machines, and food inputs to produce microwave dinners. In the following scenarios determine whether the firm's demand for labor will be relatively *more elastic*, *less elastic*, or have *no effect* on the firm's elasticity of demand for labor.

11. Labor costs comprise 85% of the firm's total costs.
12. The demand for microwave dinners is very price elastic.
13. Each dinner requires labor and machine use in fixed proportions that cannot be changed.
14. Each dinner can be produced using all labor, all machines, or any of a number of combinations of the two inputs.
15. The relevant portion of the demand curve for microwave dinners is inelastic.

Demand For Labor By A Monopolist

Suppose that the local trash removal company in the sleepy town of Tombstone is a monopoly. The output produced by this monopolist is measured in pounds of trash removed per hour. Due to the nature of the job, the trash company faces a competitive market wage rate of $30 per hour. Information on labor input, output, and price is given in this table. Complete the table and refer to the figure to answer the following questions.

L	Q	P	TR	MR	MPP$_L$	MRP	VMP	MFC
0	0	$20		XXX	XXX	XXX	XXX	XXX
1	10	19						
2	19	18						
3	27	17						
4	34	16						
5	40	15						
6	45	14						
7	49	13						
8	52	12						
9	54	11						

16. What is the numerical value (from the table) that belongs at point b?
17. What is the numerical value (from the table) that belongs at point c?
18. What is the numerical value (from the table) that belongs at point a?
19. What integer value lies between points d and e?
20. What is the amount of monopolistic exploitation of labor (in dollars) by this firm?

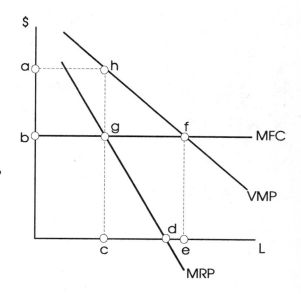

Present Value Calculations

Suppose that a tax-free lottery prize consists of 6 annual payments of $10,000. The interest rate is 8%, and the first payment begins now. (Note that this results in the last payment being made at the end of the fifth year.)

21. What is the present value of this prize (in dollars to the nearest thousand)?
22. What would happen to the present value of this prize if the interest rate used for discounting fell? (increase, decrease, no change)

Suppose that there are two investment opportunities available to you, each involving an initial outlay of $1000. The first project (Project A) will provide $10,000 each year for three years beginning one year from today. The other project (Project B) will also begin to pay one year from now and will consist of 6 annual payments of $6,000 each. Based solely on each project's present value,

23. which project would you choose at an interest rate of 5%?
24. which project would you choose if the interest rate were 10%?
25. which project would you choose if the interest rate were 20%?

Answers for HomeWork Set I-9

(a) 0	(a) 10	(a) point a	(a) Project A
(b) 1	(b) 20	(b) point b	(b) Project B
(c) 2	(c) 30	(c) point c	(c) Both projects are equally profitable
(d) 3	(d) 40	(d) point d	(d) increase
(e) 4	(e) 50	(e) point e	(e) decrease

(a) 5	(a) 60	(a) point f	(a) no change
(b) 6	(b) 70	(b) point g	(b) more elastic
(c) 7	(c) 80	(c) point h	(c) less elastic
(d) 8	(d) 90	(d) 272	(d) no effect
(e) 9	(e) 100	(e) 170	(e) need more information

HomeWork Set I-10
Market Failure and Regulation
(Chapters 12 & 17)

Externalities & Public Goods

Using the list below, which response is an example of a:

1. negative externality?
2. positive externality?
3. public good?

a. You have to pay more for coffee because an international coffee bean cartel restricts output.
b. Cheeseburgers at a national park restaurant.
c. You have a reduced risk of illness because your roommates see their doctors regularly.
d. Street lights on your block.
e. Less people choose to pursue a career in economics, increasing your future salary as an economist.

a. Service stations on a toll road.
b. Noise from a nearby party while you are trying to study.
c. Cheeseburgers at the local fast food restaurant.
d. Electricity provided by a local municipality.
e. As a result of increased demand for medical services, it costs you more to see a doctor.

Use the information in this figure, concerning production by a paper factory, to answer the following questions.

4. What is the amount (in dollars) of the marginal external costs of producing paper?
5. What is the equilibrium market price (in dollars)?
6. What is the equilibrium market quantity (in thousands of pounds)?
7. What is the socially optimal price (in dollars)?
8. What is the socially optimal quantity (in thousands of pounds)?
9. What is the amount of welfare loss (in thousands of dollars) due to the negative externality?

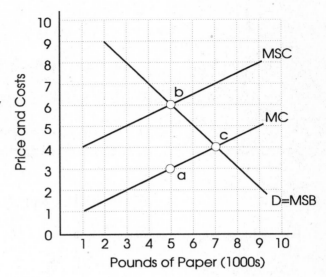

A small community consists of three people: Alice, Bob, and Pat. Their individual demands for glasses of lemonade are given in this table.

Alice		Bob		Pat	
Price	Glasses of Lemonade	Price	Glasses of Lemonade	Price	Glasses of Lemonade
$1.00	2	$1.00	1	$1.00	0
.75	3	.75	2	.75	1
.50	4	.50	3	.50	2
.25	5	.25	4	.25	4

10. What is the total quantity demanded of lemonade at a price of $0.75?
11. What is the equilibrium quantity of lemonade if the marginal cost of lemonade is constant and equal to $0.50?

Alice, Bob, and Pat want to add some exotic trees (a public good) to their community park. Individual demands for these trees is given in this table. The marginal cost of placing the trees in the park is constant and equal to $485.

Alice		Bob		Pat	
Price	Exotic Trees	Price	Exotic Trees	Price	Exotic Trees
$100.00	1	$100.00	1	$100.00	1
75.00	2	250.00	2	160.00	2
50.00	3	200.00	3	150.00	3
25.00	4	150.00	4	140.00	4

12. What is Alice's willingness to pay (in dollars) for the third tree?
13. What is the total willingness to pay (in hundreds of dollars) in this society for the third tree?
14. What is the optimal quantity of trees that should be added to the park?
15. How many exotic trees will be placed in the community park if Alice, Bob, and Pat reveal their preferences for the trees at one-half of their true valuations as given in the table?

Excess Burden Of Taxation

Use this figure, which shows a tax on cigarettes, to answer the following questions.

16. What is the amount of the tax (in dollars per pack)?
17. What is the after-tax price (in dollars) paid by consumers?
18. What is the after-tax price (in dollars) received by producers?
19. What is the amount of government tax revenues (in millions of dollars) from this tax?
20. What is the amount of the excess burden (in millions of dollars) due to this tax?

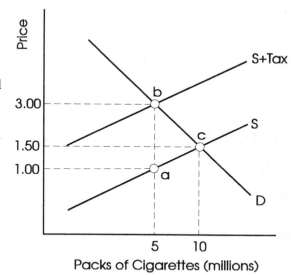

Regulating A Natural Monopoly

A natural monopoly is one in which average costs decline as output is expanded over the entire range of output. The result is that a single firm supplies the market, but the socially optimal level of output is not produced. One such natural monopoly is illustrated in this figure.

21. What is the price (in dollars) charged by the monopoly firm?
22. What regulated price (in dollars) would result in normal economic profits for the firm and ensure neither a shortage or surplus?
23. What is the socially optimal price (in dollars)?
24. By how much (in millions) does the monopoly output level fall short of the socially optimal level of output?
25. By how much (in millions) does the output level at the regulated price (from question 22) fall short of the socially optimal level of output?

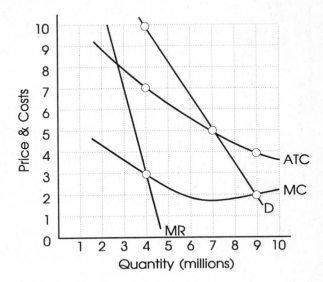

Answers for HomeWork Set I-10

(a) 0	(a) 10	(a) 0.25
(b) 1	(b) 20	(b) 0.50
(c) 2	(c) 30	(c) 0.75
(d) 3	(d) 40	(d) 25
(e) 4	(e) 50	(e) 75

(a) 5	(a) 60	(a) 140
(b) 6	(b) 70	(b) 150
(c) 7	(c) 80	(c) 160
(d) 8	(d) 90	(d) 170
(e) 9	(e) 100	(e) 250

HomeWork Set II-1
Introduction to Microeconomics
(Chapter 1)

Positive Versus Normative Analysis

Determine whether the following statements are positive or normative.

1. Interest rates were too high throughout most of the 1980s.
2. The unemployment rate was 4.3 percent last year.
3. American workers should not have to compete with cheap foreign labor.
4. There needs to be a decrease in defense spending the United States.
5. In real terms, the cost of a four-year college degree is greater now than it was 20 years ago.

Efficiency

Determine which type of efficiency (allocative, productive, distributive, or economic) is being described in the following statements.

6. The opportunity cost for a given value of output is minimized.
7. It is impossible for anyone to gain unless someone else loses.
8. The social value of output produced from given resources is maximized.
9. Specific goods are used by the people who value them relatively the most.

Graphical Analysis

Use this figure to answer the following questions.

10. Which line segment contains the ordered pair (6,4)?
11. Which line segment has a slope of -2?
12. Which line segment has a slope of 3/2?
13. Which line segment has a slope of 1/2?
14. What type of relationship is represented by line segment ef? (positive, negative, neutral)
15. Which line segment, if extended, will intercept the y axis at (0,7)?

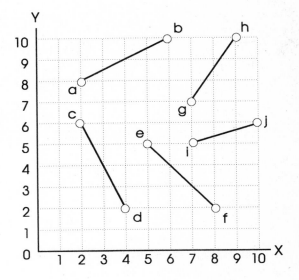

Use this figure, which depicts a hypothetical tax system, for the following questions.

16. What is the amount of tax (in thousands of dollars) for a person earning $20,000?
17. What is the amount of tax (in thousands of dollars) for a person earning $70,000?
18. What is the additional amount of tax (in thousands of dollars) that must be paid if a person's income increases from $40,000 to $50,000?
19. What is the additional amount of tax (in thousands of dollars) that must be paid if a person's income increases from $90,000 to $100,000?
20. What is the slope of the line in the figure?

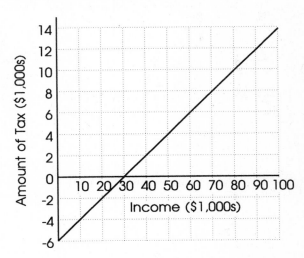

This figure shows a linear demand curve (D) and a long run average total cost curve (LRATC). You will learn more about these and other curves in the weeks ahead. For now, use your knowledge about graphs to answer the following questions based on this figure.

21. Which point corresponds to the minimum of the LRATC curve?
22. At the minimum of the LRATC curve, long run average total cost (in dollars) equals?
23. What does the slope of the LRATC curve equal at its minimum?
24. At which point is the demand curve (D) tangent to the LRATC curve?
25. What does the slope of the LRATC equal at point b?

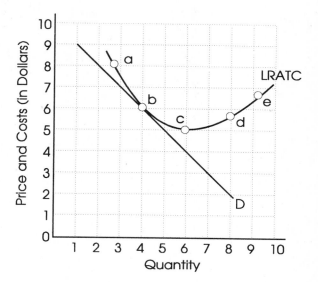

Answers for HomeWork Set II-1

(a) -6	(a) 4	(a) negative	(a) allocative
(b) -4	(b) 5	(b) positive	(b) productive
(c) -2	(c) 6	(c) neutral	(c) distributive
(d) -1	(d) 7	(d) decrease	(d) economic
(e) -1/5	(e) 8	(e) increase	(e) normative

(a) 0	(a) 9	(a) ab	(a) point a
(b) 1/5	(b) 10	(b) cd	(b) point b
(c) 1	(c) 11	(c) ef	(c) point c
(d) 2	(d) 12	(d) gh	(d) point d
(e) 3	(e) 13	(e) ij	(e) point e

HomeWork Set II-2
Opportunity Costs and Production Possibilities Analysis
(Chapter 2)

Concepts

Answer the following questions by picking the appropriate concept from this table.

1. Modern corporations are comprised of numerous departments, each responsible for a different task. Accounting, marketing, and production departments are but a few examples. The organization of a firm in this manner is an example of?

2. When Japan trades television sets for U.S. made airplanes, both countries benefit due to?

3. Suppose one night you decide to go to an all-you-can-eat spaghetti special at a local restaurant. The first serving you eat is very

a.	Queuing
b.	Brute Force
c.	The Law of Diminishing Returns
d.	Constant Opportunity Costs
e.	Decreasing Opportunity Costs
a.	Increasing Opportunity Costs
b.	Production Possibilities
c.	Random Selection
d.	The Division of Labor
e.	The Law of Comparative Advantage

satisfying, the second serving, while completely delicious, is not quite as satisfying as the first serving. The third serving makes you sick. This scenario is an example of?

4. If the production possibilities frontier were a straight line, then the production technology is characterized by?

5. For many years, eastern bloc countries such as Poland rarely relied on markets as an allocative mechanism. As a result people were often seen lining up for many city blocks waiting for such basic items as bread and toilet paper. The allocative mechanism in place in such countries was?

Opportunity Costs

Suppose that Coleen Collegiate is faced with the following trade-offs between income from work and overall grade point average (GPA) in her classes:

Hours Working per Week	Income	Hours Studying per Week	GPA
40	$400	0	0.0
30	300	10	1.6
20	200	20	2.8
10	100	30	3.6
0	0	40	4.0

6. What is Coleen's opportunity cost (in dollars) of increasing the amount of hours studying in order to earn a 3.6 GPA rather than a 2.8?
7. Is Coleen's opportunity cost of *increasing* work from 10 to 20 hours per week the same as her opportunity cost of increasing work from 20 to 30 hours per week? (yes, no)
8. Coleen's production possibilities between income and GPA exhibits (increasing, constant, decreasing) opportunity costs.

The Production Possibilities Curve

Use this figure, which illustrates the production possibilities frontier for the country of Iceolashun (a nation quite similar to the U.S.), to answer the following questions.

9. At which point are all scarce resources fully and efficiently employed?
10. Which point would require an increase in the labor force?
11. Which point represents an inefficient use of resources?
12. Which point would require an increase in the capital stock of the country?
13. Which point might be achieved by an improvement in technology?
14. Which point shows unemployment of resources?
15. What is the opportunity cost (in billions of roses) of producing 40,000 guns?

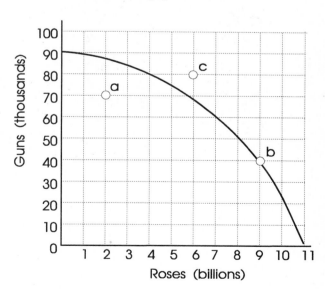

16. What is the opportunity cost (in billions of roses) of increasing gun production from 40,000 to 60,000?
17. What is the opportunity cost (in thousands of guns) of 4 billion roses?
18. What is the opportunity cost (in thousands of guns) of increasing the production of roses form 4 billion to 9 billion?
19. Does this production possibilities frontier illustrate constant, increasing, or decreasing opportunity costs?

Comparative Advantage And The PPF

Two countries, Transylvania and Tasmania, each produce milk and cookies with constant opportunity costs. Use this figure, which shows the production possibilities frontiers for these two countries, to answer the following questions.

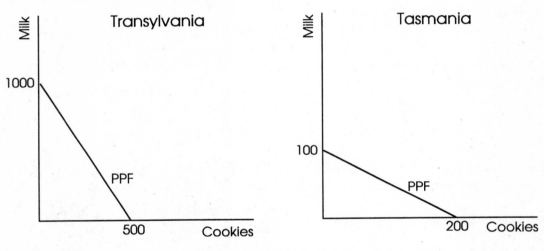

20. The opportunity cost of a cookie in Transylvania equals how many units of milk?
21. The opportunity cost of a cookie in Tasmania equals how many units of milk?
22. Which country has a comparative advantage in cookie production?
23. Which country has an absolute advantage in production of milk and cookies?
24. Is it possible for both countries to benefit from specialization and trade? (yes, no)
25. If these regions trade, which country will export milk?

Answers for HomeWork Set II-2

(a) 0	(a) 60	(a) point a	(a) Queuing
(b) 1/3	(b) 70	(b) point b	(b) Brute Force
(c) 1/2	(c) 80	(c) point c	(c) The Law of Diminishing Returns
(d) 2	(d) 90	(d) yes	(d) Constant Opportunity Costs
(e) 3	(e) 100	(e) no	(e) Decreasing Opportunity Costs
(a) 10	(a) 110	(a) increasing	(a) Increasing Opportunity Costs
(b) 20	(b) Transylvania	(b) decreasing	(b) Production Possibilities
(c) 30	(c) Tasmania	(c) constant	(c) Random Selection
(d) 40	(d) neither	(d) positive	(d) The Division of Labor
(e) 50	(e) both	(e) negative	(e) The Law of Comparative Advantage

HomeWork Set II-3
Supply and Demand Analysis
(Chapters 3 & 4)

Changes in Supply Vs Changes in Quantity Supplied

Use this figure and response column to answer the questions below. (Each scenario should cause no response, a movement from **a** to points **e** or **d**, or a shift from **a** to **b** or **c**.)

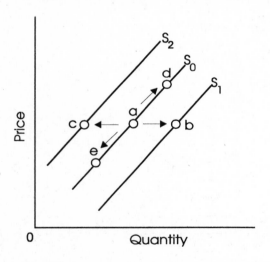

POSSIBLE RESPONSE

a. no response
b. increase in supply (shift to b)
c. decrease in supply (shift to c)
d. movement to d (increase in quantity supplied)
e. movement to e (decrease in quantity supplied)

Starting in each instance at point **a**, what will happen to supply when:

1. New firms enter the industry?
2. Price increases?
3. The price of a substitute in production increases?
4. Price decreases?
5. The price of an input increases?
6. Losses cause some firms to exit the industry?
7. New technology reduces the costs of production?

Shortage, Surplus, and Equilibrium

Use this figure to answer the following questions.

8. The quantity demanded at a price of $50 is?
9. By how many units will quantity demanded exceed quantity supplied if the price is $30?
10. The price (in dollars) at which quantity supplied equals 30 is?
11. The price (in dollars) at which a surplus will occur is?

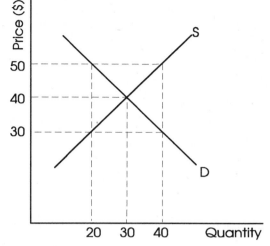

Use this figure, which illustrates the peanut market, to answer the following questions. For each question assume that the market begins at D_0 and S_0.

12. What will be the new equilibrium price if peanut workers receive a wage increase?
13. What will be the new equilibrium quantity if eating peanuts is predicted to prevent AIDS while at the same time new endangered species protections greatly reduce the land available for peanut production?
14. What will be the new equilibrium quantity if the price of U-Haul trailer rentals increases by 50%?
15. What is the new equilibrium price if peanuts are an inferior good and real income per capita declines?

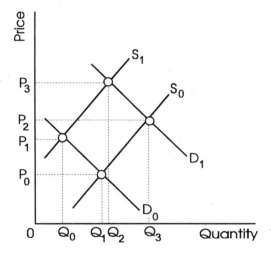

Price Floors and Price Ceilings

This figure represents a labor market for unskilled workers. Currently the government has set a minimum wage of W_3 in this labor market, but is considering elimination of the minimum wage legislation.

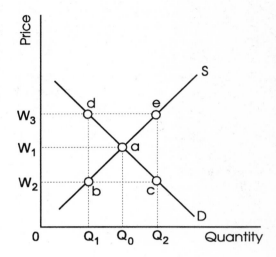

16. Is a minimum wage a price floor or a price ceiling?
17. The number of jobs available could be increased if the minimum wage was eliminated because quantity demanded of labor would increase from Q_1 to?
18. An elimination of the minimum wage in this market should decrease the quantity supplied of labor from Q_2 to?
19. The horizontal distance between which two points measures the possible unemployment caused by the minimum wage of W_3?
20. Will some workers be better off if a minimum wage is eliminated? (yes/no)
21. Will some workers be worse off if a minimum wage of W_3 is eliminated? (yes/no)
22. What will be the market wage rate after the market adjusts to an elimination of the minimum wage?

Assume the market wage is currently W_2 and no minimum wage laws are in effect.

23. What should happen to the wage rate over time? (no change, increase, decrease)

Question for Thought
Which workers would oppose a reduction or elimination of the minimum wage? (Who might be made worse off by the elimination of the minimum wage?)

Fleeing stagnation in California, economic refugees have descended in record numbers upon the towns and cities of the Rocky Mountains. Accompanying the rapid rise in population has been a concomitant rise in the prices paid for rental housing. Long time residents in many towns are beginning to call for rent controls so that living remains "affordable" in their town.

24. Are rent controls a price ceiling or a price floor?
25. Who will benefit from the rent controls?

Answers for HomeWork Set II-3

(a) yes
(b) no
(c) W_1
(d) W_2
(e) W_3

(a) 20
(b) 25
(c) 30
(d) 80
(e) 60

(a) price floor
(b) price ceiling
(c) Q_1
(d) Q_0
(e) Q_2

(a) 0
(b) 10
(c) increase
(d) decrease
(e) no change

(a) 40
(b) 50
(c) de
(d) ec
(e) bc

(a) Q_3
(b) P_0
(c) P_1
(d) P_2
(e) P_3

(a) all renters
(b) all landlords
(c) all renters able to find apartments at controlled prices
(d) equilibrium price
(e) market price

HomeWork Set II-4
Elasticity, Tax Burdens, and Consumer Choice
(Chapters 5 & 6)

Price Elasticity and Total Revenue

This table illustrates the monthly demand schedule for Betty's Burlap Baggage (BBB), a "one size fits all uses" travel bag.

Price	Quantity	Price Elasticity	Total Revenue
20	100	xxx	
18	150		
16	200		
14	250		
12	300		
10	350		
8	400		

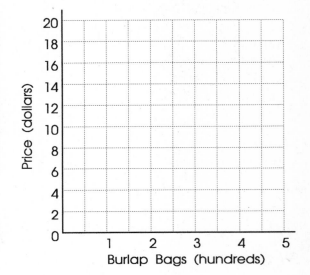

a. Plot the demand curve in the figure.
b. Fill in the price elasticity column, using the mid-points formula. Use *absolute values*, and round all calculations to the nearest tenth (.1)
c. Fill in the total revenue column.

1. The price elasticity of demand between $18 and $16 is?
2. Between $18 and $16, is the demand for Betty's baggage elastic, inelastic, or unitarily elastic?
3. What happens to the price elasticity of demand as price falls? (increases, decreases, or doesn't change)
4. The price elasticity of demand between $10 and $8 is?.
5. Between $10 and $8, is the demand for Betty's baggage elastic, inelastic, or unitarily elastic?
6. What is Betty's total revenue when she sells her bags at $12 each?
7. When Betty is on the elastic portion of her demand curve, what happens to total revenue when she raises the price of her bags? (increases, decreases, or doesn't change)
8. When Betty is on the inelastic portion of her demand curve, what happens to total revenue when she raises the price of her bags? (increases, decreases, or doesn't change)

Use these figures to help you answer the following questions.

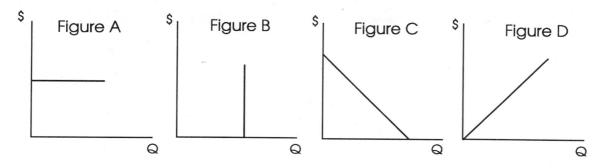

9. The Denver Broncos always have a sell out crowd at their 75,000 seat Mile High Stadium in Denver, Colorado. Which of the figures best represents the supply curve for Broncos tickets at Mile High Stadium?
10. What is the value of the price elasticity of supply in question nine?
11. Connie runs a small contracting firm. She finds that the market price for a new family room addition is $4000.00 and that she can sell as many of these room additions as she desires at this price. Which of the figures best represents the demand curve for room additions facing Connie's firm?
12. What is the value of the price elasticity of demand in question eleven?

Elasticity and Tax Burdens

Who bears the economic burden (consumers or sellers) if a tax is levied in:

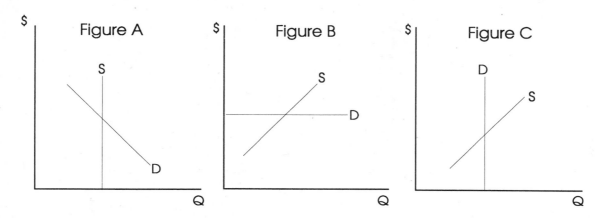

13. Figure A?
14. Figure B?
15. Figure C?

Many economists and environmentalists advocate raising taxes on gasoline and other fossil fuels to reduce pollution. The theory is that higher pump prices will lead to reduced driving, increased car-pooling, increased ridership on public transportation and thus, reduced emissions.

As this figure shows, Americans consume about 450 million gallons of gasoline a day. Current estimates put the short-run elasticity for gasoline at -.20 and a long-run elasticity of approximately -1.5. Both the short-run and long-run supply of gasoline are assumed to be perfectly elastic at current market prices ($1.25 per gallon).

Assume that Congress levies a 50 cent per gallon tax on gasoline. Draw the new supply curve in the figure, and answer the following questions.

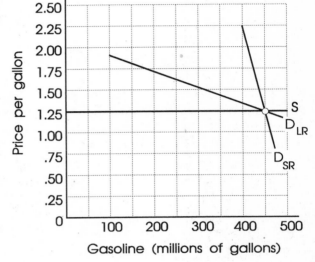

16. What will be the short-run price of gasoline after imposition of the tax?
17. Who actually pays the tax (the economic incidence) in this case, consumers or sellers?
18. After the imposition of the tax, what happens to the quantity of gasoline consumed as we move from the short run to the long run? (increases, decreases, or doesn't change)
19. If the goal of the tax is pollution reduction, will the tax be more effective in the short run or the long run?
20. If the goal of the tax is additional tax revenue, will the tax be more effective in the short run or the long run?

Consumer Equilibrium

In the following scenarios determine whether you will maximize your utility by a) purchasing more candy bars and fewer soft drinks, b) purchasing more soft drinks and fewer candy bars, or c) not changing your present consumption of soft drinks and candy bars.

21. Your marginal utility from a 50 cent soft drink is 100 utils and your marginal utility from a 35 cent candy bar is 80 utils.
22. Your marginal utility from a 75 cent soft drink is 225 utils and your marginal utility from a 60 cent candy bar is 180 utils.
23. Your marginal utility from a $1 soft drink is 375 utils and your marginal utility from a 75 cent candy bar is 265 utils.

Consumer Surplus

Use this figure, which shows your demand for MindCandy --an IQ booster, to answer the following questions.

24. If MindCandy sells for $3 a bar what is your consumer surplus from the second bar you purchase?
25. If MindCandy sells for $2 a bar, what does your entire consumer surplus equal? (Assume that MindCandy can be sold in fractions of a bar.)

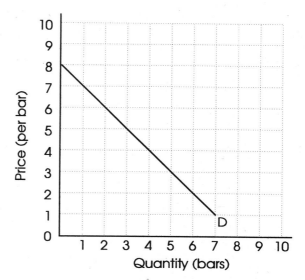

Answers for HomeWork Set II-4

(a) a
(b) b
(c) c
(d) elastic
(e) inelastic

(a) $3,200
(b) $3,500
(c) $3,600
(d) consumers
(e) sellers

(a) Figure A
(b) Figure B
(c) Figure C
(d) Figure D
(e) 3.8

(a) $1
(b) $2
(c) $3
(d) $4
(e) $5

(a) unitarily elastic
(b) increases
(c) decreases
(d) doesn't change
(e) midpoint

(a) $1.25
(b) $1.50
(c) $1.75
(d) short run
(e) long run

(a) 2.4
(b) 1.7
(c) 1.2
(d) .8
(e) .6

(a) $6
(b) $18
(c) $36
(d) 0
(e) infinity

HomeWork Set II-5
Production and Costs
(Chapter 8)

Short-Run Average and Marginal Product

Tiring of life in the hustle-bustle world of high finance, you decide to return to a simpler life, and move to South Park, a small mountain town inhabited primarily by artisans. Rather soon, your new friends in the woods draw you into their bird carving guild. They are awed with your knowledge of finance and economics(?), and want you to establish a co-op to sell their wood carved eagles. Remembering that your kindergarten teacher remarked that you had a way with crayons, you decide to embark on this business adventure. The first thing you decide to uncover is the rate of productivity of the artists available for the new co-op, called Mountain Sky Carvers of DaMountains (MSCD). The number of carvers and their monthly output when working under one roof and supervision is defined as follows:

Labor	Output	APP_L	MPP_L
1	8		
2	17		
3	24		
4	30		
5	35		
6	39		
7	42		
8	44		
9	45		
10	44		
11	41		

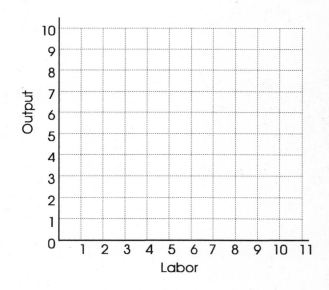

Complete the table and graph APP_L and MPP_L on the figure.

1. What is the APP_L if MSCD produces 45 carved eagles per month?
2. What is the MPP_L of the third worker?
3. What accounts for the fact that MPP_L falls when the sixth artist is hired? (artistic differences, diminishing returns, or economies of scale)
4. At what employment level is average physical product the highest?
5. At what employment level is marginal physical product the highest?

Short-Run Costs of Production

At the first meeting of Mountain Sky Carvers of DaMountains (MSCD), you and your colleagues decide to lease a warehouse that can be used as a manufacturing facility for the co-op's carved eagles. The cost of this facility is $1,000 per month. Even though this is a small mountain community composed mainly of artisans, labor is not cheap and artists are only willing to work for $2,000 a month.

Copy your answers for the APP_L and the MPP_L from the table above into this table. Fill in all the remaining columns, and round all your answers to two decimal places (cents). Plot AVC, AFC, ATC and MC on the figure.

Labor	Output	APP_L	MPP_L	TVC	AVC	TC	ATC	AFC	MC
1	8								
2	17								
3	24								
4	30								
5	35								
6	39								
7	42								
8	44								
9	45								
10	44								
11	41								

6. What is AVC when output equals 45 birds (in dollars)?
7. AFC for an output of 42 birds (nearest dollar) is?.
8. What is the MC when output equals 39 carved eagles?
9. Minimum average total cost occurs when how many units of labor are employed?
10. When 8 units of labor are employed marginal cost is equal to ?
11. Average variable costs are equal to $364 at what level of employment?

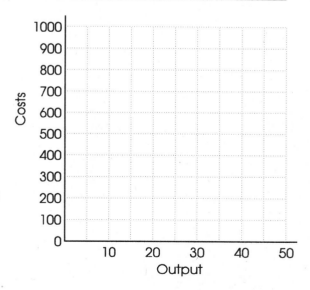

Costs of Production -- Graphical Analysis

Use this figure, which depicts costs and output for a small firm, to answer the following questions. Assume output is 25,000 units.

12. Total costs (in thousands of dollars) are?
13. Total variable costs (in thousands of dollars) are?
14. Total fixed costs (in thousands of dollars) are?
15. Is this firm operating in the short run or in the long run?
16. How much profit (TR - TC) does the firm make by producing 25,000 units and selling those units at $8 per unit (in thousands of dollars)?
17. How much is AFC (in dollars) at 25,000 units?
18. What is the MC (in dollars) at this output?

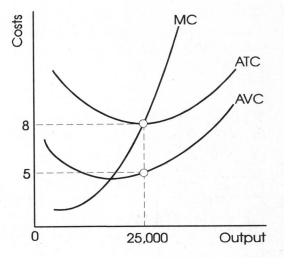

Long-Run Costs of Production

Plot the three short run average total cost (ATC) curves in this table on the figure. Also plot the long run average total cost (LRATC) curve associated with these three short run ATC.

Q	ATC$_1$	ATC$_2$	ATC$_3$
0	--	--	--
100	25	--	--
200	17	--	--
300	15	--	--
400	17	15	--
500	19	12	--
600	25	10	--
700	--	12	20
800	--	14	17
900	--	15	14
1,000	--	20	13
1,100	--	--	14
1,200	--	--	20

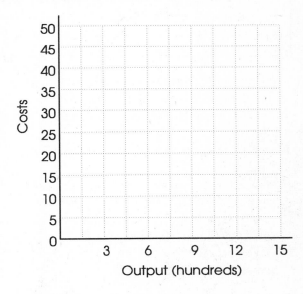

19. Below what output does this LRATC curve exhibit economies of scale?
20. Above what output does this LRATC curve exhibit diseconomies of scale?

Diminishing, Constant, And Increasing Returns

Use these figures, which depict various total product (TP) curves, to answer the following questions.

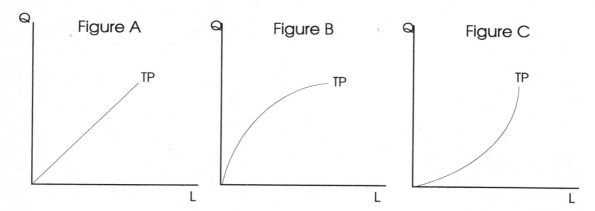

21. Which of the three figures shows a total product curve which exhibits increasing marginal returns?
22. For which of the three figures would the associated MC curve be upward sloping?

Panel A of this figure shows a typical total product (TP) curve. Plot the associated MPP_L and APP_L in panel b. Label points a, b, and c on your MPP_L and APP_L curves.

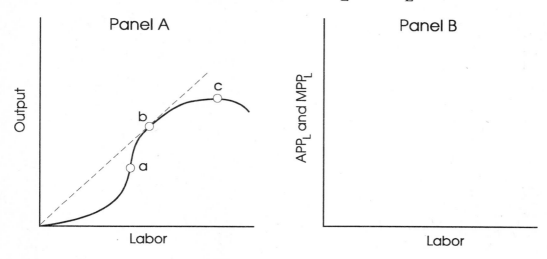

23. At which point (a, b, or c) is the $MPP_L = 0$?
24. At point b is MPP_L less than, greater than, or equal to APP_L?
25. At what point is MC at a minimum?

Answers for HomeWork Set II-5

(a) 0	(a) 20	(a) 400	(a) Figure A
(b) 1	(b) 24	(b) 500	(b) Figure B
(c) 2	(c) 50	(c) less than	(c) Figure C
(d) 3	(d) 75	(d) 700	(d) diminishing returns
(e) 4	(e) 100	(e) 900	(e) economies of scale

(a) 5	(a) 125	(a) 1,000	(a) a
(b) 6	(b) 175	(b) 600	(b) b
(c) 7	(c) 200	(c) greater than	(c) c
(d) 8	(d) 90	(d) equal to	(d) short run
(e) 9	(e) 300	(e) artistic differences	(e) long run

HomeWork Set II-6
The Competitive Ideal
(Chapter 9)

Competitive Profit Maximization -- MSCD is Launched

Convinced that a fortune can be made selling wood carved eagles, Mountain Sky Carvers of DaMountains (MSCD) is launched. Top management of MSCD has their second meeting where Mark E. Ting, the Sales Manager announces that he has discovered numerous mountain communities across the country where wood carved eagles are produced. While there are clearly differences in the size, type and quality of eagles carved, the market is quite competitive and that within a reasonable range a solid market exists. Given the type, quality and size of eagles MSCD carves, he feels confident that he can sell all MSCD produces at $500.00 per carving.

Fill in the remainder of this table, which lists monthly employment, costs and profit at MSCD.

Labor	Output	AVC	ATC	MC	TR	MR	TC	Profit
1	8	250.00	375.00	250.00				
2	17	235.29	294.12	222.22				
3	24	250.00	291.67	285.71				
4	30	266.67	300.00	333.33				
5	35	285.71	314.29	400.00				
6	39	307.69	333.33	500.00				
7	42	333.33	357.14	667.67				
8	44	363.64	386.36	1,000.00				

Note: If two outputs yield the same profits (losses) use the *highest* output for your answer.
1. What is the profit maximizing output?
2. What does marginal cost (MC) equal (in dollars) at the profit maximizing output?
3. What does total revenue (TR) equal (in dollars) at the profit maximizing output?
4. What do total costs (TC) equal (in dollars) at the profit maximizing output?
5. What does monthly profit (Π) equal (in dollars) at the profit maximizing output?
6. How many artists will be hired to produce the profit maximizing output?
7. What do total fixed costs (TFC) equal (in dollars)?

Plot your values for AVC, ATC, MC, and MR from the table above in this figure. Shade in the area representing MSCD's profit.

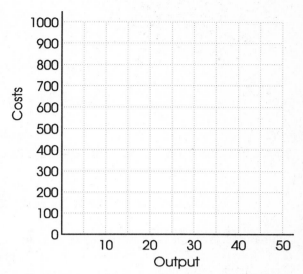

Problems in the Mountains

Mountain Sky Carvers of DaMountains is a thriving business, providing you with something to do during the day, and a gross income of $78,000 a year. It seems you have it made! But cool winds of change are blowing. South Park is becoming a popular area to tourists and a Japanese consortium has announced it will be building and operating the worlds largest water skiing, camping, hiking and general all-around fun area within twelve months. Unfortunately, your one year lease expires in two months and the landlord has decided to raise MSCD's rent to $3,000 per month (reflecting the general increase in expectations for economic growth in South Park). In addition, your Sales Manager, Mark E. Ting, has indicated that MSCD will start to incur monthly fixed sales expenses of $100.

8. How much will MSCD's monthly fixed costs be (in dollars), once the new lease goes into effect?

Complete this table, using MSCD's new monthly fixed costs (from question 8). Where appropriate, you can simply copy your answers from the previous table. The market price for carved eagles is still $500 each. Plot the new ATC curve, and shade in the area showing MSCD's profit on the above figure.

Labor	Output	TVC	AVC	ATC	MC	TR	MR	TC	Profit
1	8	2,000							
2	17	4,000							
3	24	6,000							
4	30	8,000							
5	35	10,000							
6	39	12,000							
7	42	14,000							
8	44	16,000							

Note: If two outputs yield the same profits (losses) use the *highest* output for your answer.
  9. What does MC equal (in dollars) at the profit maximizing output?
  10. What is the equilibrium level of output where profits are maximized?
  11. What does monthly profit equal (in dollars) at the profit maximizing output?

After you sign a new lease, your employees ask for a meeting. They point out that with the new developments in South Park, they can now make more money carving trinkets for the new tourist traps that are sure to follow. You want MSCD to continue in business, so you increase monthly wages (your only variable cost) by $500 to $2,500 per month.

Complete this table based on your new costs. Fixed costs and the market price of carved eagles ($500) have not changed, so copy from the previous table where appropriate. Plot the new ATC, AVC, MC and MR curves in the figure below.

Labor	Output	TVC	AVC	ATC	MC	TR	MR	TC	Profit
1	8								
2	17								
3	24								
4	30								
5	35								
6	39								
7	42								
8	44								

Note: If two outputs yield the same profits (losses) use the *highest* output for your answer.

12. What does MC equal (in dollars) at the profit maximizing output?
13. Given these new developments, what is the new profit maximizing output?
14. What does monthly profit (in dollars) equal?
15. How many artists will be hired to produce the profit maximizing output?
16. Will other artisans be tempted to get into the carved eagle business? (yes, no)

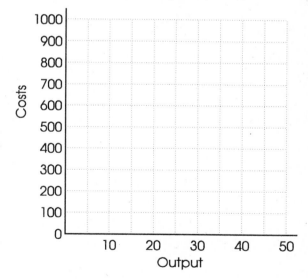

Tough Decisions in South Park

Six months into the new lease, the bottom falls out of the market for wood carved eagles. Russian entrepreneurs find wood carving is an excellent activity during the long winters and find plenty of cheap labor. Trade agreements with the United States enable them to export eagles to the U.S. increasing supplies and causing prices to plummet to $360 per eagle.

Complete this table. Since market price is the only thing that has changed, you will only need to recalculate the columns which concern revenue and profit.

Labor	Output	AVC	ATC	MC	TR	MR	TC	Profit
1	8							
2	17							
3	24							
4	30							
5	35							
6	39							
7	42							
8	44							

17. How much (in dollars) would MSCD lose if it shut down?
18. Assume that you hire 3 people, what is the MC (in dollars) at this output?
19. How large are monthly losses?
20. Given these developments, what is equilibrium output?
21. Do you think that MSCD will be operating in the long run if costs and market price remain unchanged? (yes, no)

As if the Russian invasion wasn't enough, Mexican woodcarvers get into the act and prices fall to $250 per eagle.

Complete this table. Once again, since market price is the only thing that has changed, you will only need to recalculate the columns which concern revenue and profit.

Labor	Output	AVC	ATC	MC	TR	MR	TC	Profit
1	8							
2	17							
3	24							
4	30							
5	35							
6	39							
7	42							
8	44							

22. How much (in dollars) would MSCD lose if it shut down?
23. Given this new price, what is equilibrium output?
24. How large are monthly losses (in dollars)?
25. How many artists will be hired to produce the profit maximizing output?

Answers for HomeWork Set II-6

(a) 0	(a) 20	(a) 2,000	(a) 10,000
(b) 1	(b) 24	(b) 1,960	(b) 12,000
(c) 2	(c) 30	(c) 3,000	(c) 13,000
(d) 3	(d) 35	(d) 3,100	(d) 15,000
(e) 4	(e) 39	(e) 4,000	(e) 17,000

(a) 5	(a) 40	(a) 4,400	(a) 19,000
(b) 6	(b) 357	(b) 5,000	(b) 19,500
(c) 7	(c) 500	(c) 6,000	(c) 21,000
(d) 8	(d) 1,000	(d) 6,500	(d) yes
(e) 9	(e) 1,900	(e) 7,500	(e) no

HomeWork Set II-7
Monopoly
(Chapter 10)

Capitalism Re-awakens in South Park

After losing your tusche in the woodcarved eagle market, you decided to go back to your prior life of hunting and gathering in the mountains. Life continued as usual (admittedly at a low standard of living ... but you were happy?) until one day you discovered a process to turn wildflower buds into a malted drink that was a cross between Pepsi (or possibly Coke depending on your tastebuds) and beer. Your new concoction, as you discovered, made an excellent breakfast drink (and a good coffee replacement) that made the drudgery of work go by quickly, but seemed to prolong the pleasure of recreation almost endlessly.

Despite your prior business reversals, your friends (who by now would line up in the morning for a shot of "Overjoy Juice") began to encourage you to "have another go" at capitalism. Unable to stand the pressure, you founded Overjoy Juice Transcontinental (OJT) to process and market Overjoy Juice (OJ for short). After discussing your plans with local attorney Wendy Holmes, you recognized that patents could be reverse engineered, so you decided to keep the preparation of OJ a secret between you and your significant other. This you felt would cement your apparent monopoly on OJ.

Use this figure, which provides monthly data on the market and costs associated with producing OJ, to answer the following questions.

1. What output will you produce (in thousands) in order to maximize profit?
2. What price (in dollars) will you charge (per cup of OJ) in order to maximize profit?
3. What will your monthly total revenue (in thousands of dollars) equal?
4. What will your monthly total costs (in thousands of dollars) equal?
5. What will your monthly profit (in thousands of dollars) equal?
6. What will your monthly profit per cup (in dollars) equal?

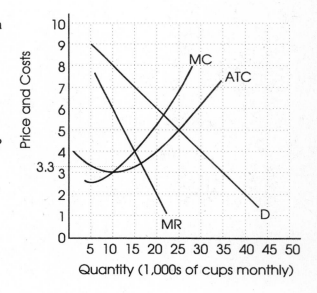

7. Given your present position, do you think that you will want to continue producing OJ in the long run? (yes, no, can't determine)
8. Will other entrepreneurs be tempted to produce a breakfast drink that is similar to OJ? (yes, no, can't determine)
9. At the profit maximizing level of output, will the demand for OJ be elastic, inelastic or unitarily elastic?

Unfortunately (for you), other firms "crack" OJ's secret recipe and turn the industry into a model of pure competition. Surprisingly, however, your company's cost curves represent the most efficient method of producing OJ (even in the long run), so all your competitors have cost curves which are identical to your cost curves.

10. Now that the industry is purely competitive, what will your monthly output (in thousands) equal?
11. What price (in dollars) will you now charge for a cup of OJ?
12. What will your monthly profit (in thousands of dollars) equal?
13. If the market demand for OJ (at the current competitive price) equals 1 million cups per month, how many firms will comprise the industry?

Sphinx Tours

Your up-tight friend H. M. Roy Dees (known as Roydees) suggests that you join his travel business, Sphinx Tours. Roydees knows you are about to finish (?) a course in Microeconomics, and therefore solicits your advice. Sphinx Tours' business involves setting up short Middle East tours, primarily to Egypt. These tours handle everything from beginning to end, so that clients may enjoy a hassle-free vacation. Sphinx Tours is very specialized and has distinguished itself with close ties to the best Egyptian guides, and as such enjoys substantial market power in this limited area. Anyone thinking about a tour to the Middle East invariably call Sphinx Tours first.

Last year Roydees hired a marketing research firm to examine the annual demand for Middle East tours. As part of their report, the marketing research firm indicated that for a 10 day tour to Egypt, no one was willing to travel at $4,000 or above. The firm noted, however, that for every $500 drop in the price of tours, 100 additional people will book tours until the tour price is $3,000. After a $3,000 tour price is reached, 200 additional people will book tours for every $500 reduction in the price of a tour.

Roydees's Sphinx Tours operation is run out of his house, and excluding telephone fees (which are minimal), costs consist exclusively of variable costs per person on the tour of $1,000. These costs cover all tour expenses including transportation, hotel fees, food, overseas contracts with tour guides, etc..., and thus MC = ATC = $1,000. Roydees has been booking 800 tours a year at $1,500 per tour, and earning $400,000 a year in profit. He is pleased with his income, but like all entrepreneurs, he would like to earn more if possible. Roydees is not, however, willing to expand his business and leave his house.

Graph a) the demand curve for Middle East tours, b) the marginal revenue curve associated with this demand curve, and c) Sphinx Tour's marginal cost and average total cost curves on the figure. Note: Since the demand curve is kinked, the MR curve will be kinked as well. Further, remember that graphically, the MR curve bisects the demand curve (for all prices, MR is located at a point where quantity is half that of demand. Use the graph you generate to answer the following questions.

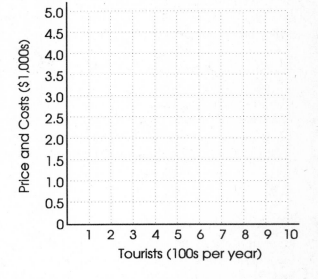

14. Is Roydees operating on the elastic, inelastic, or unitarily elastic portion of his demand curve?
15. What price (in dollars) would you suggest that Roydees charge to maximize profits?
16. How many individuals (in hundreds) would annually purchase tours at the profit maximizing price?
17. How much annual profit (in thousands of dollars) would Roydees earn at the profit maximizing price?
18. How much additional profit (in thousands of dollars) would Roydees earn by following your suggestion?

As you continue to examine the report from the marketing consultants, you discover that Roydees actually acquired additional valuable information aside from an estimate of the total demand for Middle East tours--demand for seniors (over 65) and non-seniors (less than 65) was also compiled. Non-seniors were least flexible in their demands because of employment considerations, but were willing to pay higher prices. More specifically, non-seniors were unwilling to pay $4,000 or above for a tour, but each $500 price decline resulted in 100 additional non-seniors booking a tour. Seniors, on the other hand, were more flexible (since job are not a constraint), but more price conscious. Seniors would not pay $3,000 or above for a tour, but each $500 price decline would result in 100 additional seniors booking a tour.

Plot the demand and marginal revenue curves for both seniors and non-seniors in the figure, then answer the following questions.

19. Should Roydees charge seniors and non-seniors different prices? (yes, no, can't determine)
20. What price (in dollars) should Roydees charge non-seniors in order to maximize profits?
21. How many non-seniors (in hundreds) will book tours at the profit-maximizing price?
22. What price (in dollars) should Roydees charge seniors in order to maximize profits?
23. How many seniors (in hundreds) will book tours at the profit-maximizing price?
24. What will Roydee's annual profit (in thousands of dollars) equal if he charges the profit maximizing price to seniors and non-seniors?
25. By how much will differentiating between seniors and non-seniors increase Roydee's profit? (in thousands of dollars)

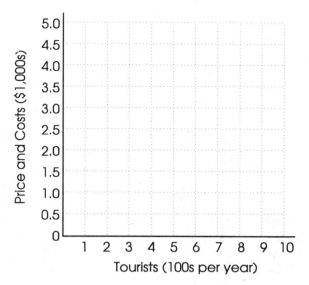

Answers for HomeWork Set II-7

(a) 0	(a) 10	(a) 105	(a) 2,000
(b) 1	(b) 15	(b) 100	(b) 2,250
(c) 2	(c) 25	(c) 200	(c) 2,500
(d) 3	(d) 40	(d) 300	(d) 3,000
(e) 3.7	(e) 49.5	(e) 225	(e) elastic

(a) 4	(a) 50	(a) 150	(a) inelastic
(b) 5	(b) 55.5	(b) 500	(b) unitarily elastic
(c) 6	(c) 65.5	(c) 525	(c) yes
(d) 7	(d) 70	(d) 625	(d) no
(e) 8	(e) 75	(e) 650	(e) can't determine

HomeWork Set II-8
Monopolistic Competition,
Oligopoly, and Strategic Behavior
(Chapter 11)

Market Structure

In the following questions determine if the market structure is pure competition, monopoly, oligopoly, or monopolistic competition.

1. In which market structure does the demand curve for the firm coincide with the market demand curve?
2. Firms in which market structure have no monopoly power?
3. Which market structure is most likely to have a cartel?
4. In which market structure, besides pure competition, will the firm(s) be in long run equilibrium when the demand curve for each firm is tangent to the firm's long run average cost curve?
5. In which market structure is conscious interdependence most important?
6. Which type of market structure is most likely to arise through horizontal merger?

Use this figure to answer the following questions.

7. Which demand curve will a pure competitor face?
8. At what price would a firm in a monopolistic competitive industry be in long run equilibrium?
9. At which output does MR = MC for a firm with monopoly power?
10. Which output and price combination represents the efficient output/price combination for the given cost curves?

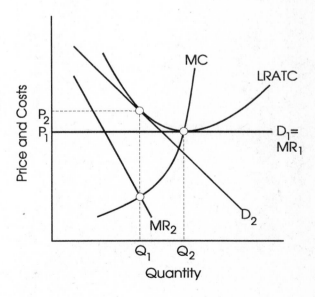

Game Theory

Jack and Jill have been indicted for fraud in connection with a land deal that led directly to the failure of a Savings and Loan Association. Prosecutors' of the case have only have enough evidence to convict each party of a misdemeanor (one year in prison) without a confession. Prosecutors are keeping Jack and Jill isolated during questioning in hopes of coaxing a confession (to ensure a felony conviction) from one or both. This table shows the expected payoff in terms of potential sentences for each party [payoffs are (Jill,Jack) and 0 means that they go free].

11. What is the expected sentence (in years) for Jill, if Jack confesses and Jill holds out?
12. What is the dominant strategy for Jill?
13. What is the Nash equilibrium in the above game?

		Jack	
		Confess	Hold Out
Jill	Confess	-3,-3	0,-6
	Hold Out	-6,0	-1,-1

14. If Jack and Jill can be effectively kept from communicating, is the game cooperative or noncooperative?
15. If Jack and Jill could communicate and enforce any agreement made between them, what would be the sentencing outcome?

The Kinked Demand Curve Model

Use this figure to answer the following questions.

16. What price will this firm charge for its output if the relevant MC curve is MC_1?
17. What price will the firm charge if marginal costs increase at each output level from MC_1 to MC_2?
18. In this model does the increase in marginal costs lead to an increase in price? (yes, no)
19. This model attempts to explain the behavior of firms in which type of market structure? (pure competition, monopolistic competition, oligopoly, or monopoly)
20. Can this model explain price rigidity? (yes, no)
21. Can this model explain how the equilibrium price is established or how prices change? (yes, no)

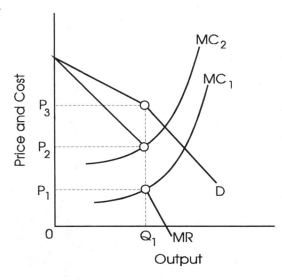

Cartels

A well known professor of economics gives multiple choice exams each semester. He curves the exams by giving the maximum possible points to the high score on the exam. For example, if a 30 question exam is worth 300 points and the top score in the class is 27, then each question is worth 300/27 = 11.11 points. Grades are then awarded as follows: 90% or better = A, 80% or better = B, 70% or better = C, 60% or better = D and below 60% =F.

22. Could the students form a cartel to ensure that each student received an A for the exam?
    (yes, no)
23. Would a student who was concerned with relative class standing have an incentive to cheat?
    (yes, no)
24. Is it likely that such a cartel would be successful in a large class? (yes, no)
25. If the students form a successful cartel, what grade would each student receive on the exam?

Answers for HomeWork Set II-8

(a) pure competition	(a) 0	(a) D_1	(a) A
(b) monopoly	(b) 1	(b) D_2	(b) B
(c) oligopoly	(c) 3	(c) Q_1	(c) C
(d) monopolistic competition	(d) 6	(d) Q_2	(d) D
(e) confess	(e) 9	(e) Q_1, P_2	(e) F

(a) hold out	(a) 12	(a) Q_2, P_1	(a) yes
(b) confess, confess	(b) 15	(b) -3, -3	(b) no
(c) confess, hold out	(c) 20	(c) 0, -6	(c) P_1
(d) hold out, confess	(d) cooperative	(d) -6, 0	(d) P_2
(e) hold out, hold out	(e) noncooperative	(e) -1, -1	(e) P_3

HomeWork Set II-9
Labor Markets

Competitive Labor Markets

This table shows a production schedule for a firm that operates in competitive markets for both output and labor. The current price of the manufactured good is $2, and the wage rate is $6 per hour. Complete the table (L = number of workers, Q = output per hour, MPP_L = marginal physical product of labor, MRP = marginal revenue product of labor, and MFC = marginal factor cost), graph the firm's marginal revenue product (MRP) and marginal factor cost (MFC) curves in the figure, and answer the following questions.

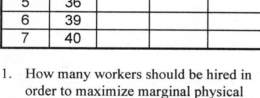

L	Q	MPP_L	MRP	MFC
1	3			
2	10			
3	20			
4	29			
5	36			
6	39			
7	40			

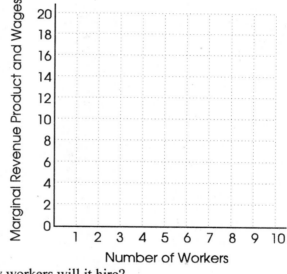

1. How many workers should be hired in order to maximize marginal physical product?

2. What is the value of the marginal product, VMP, (in dollars) when marginal physical product is at its maximum.

3. If this firm is a profit maximizer, how many workers will it hire?

4. What does MRP equal (in dollars) at the profit maximizing level of output?

Assume that the wage rate increases to $14 an hour.

5. How does the wage increase affect the demand for labor? (increase, decrease, no change)

6. How many workers will the firm hire at the new wage rate if it wishes to maximizes profit?

Assume that the wage rate is once again $6 per hour, but that the price of the firm's product rises to $6 per unit.

7. How does the increase in the product price affect the demand for labor? (increase, decrease, no change)
8. How many workers should the firm hire at the new product price in order to maximize profit?
9. Who determines the wage rate the firm will pay a worker? (the firm, workers, the market)
10. A firm maximizes profits when it hires additional workers until? (MR = MC, MRP = MFC, or S = D)

Investment in Human Capital

Use this figure, which shows the potential earnings profile for Tanya Typical, to answer the following questions

11. If Tanya decides to go to college, how old will she be before she earns as much as she would have had she entered the labor force right after high school?
12. Which area (A, B, or C) represents the direct out of pocket costs associated with obtaining a college degree?
13. Does area A represent the only opportunity costs associated with obtaining a college degree? (yes, no, can't tell)

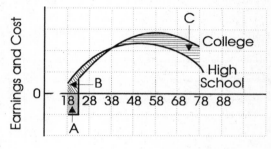

14. If lifetime earnings are the only consideration, what should Tanya do? (attend college, start work after high school, be a slacker)
15. If Tanya was indifferent to attending college or working right after high school because both options would result in the same lifetime earnings, which option would confer the greatest benefits on society?

Labor Market Efficiency

Use this figure to answer the following questions. Assume that markets are perfectly competitive and that no externalities exist.

16. At what wage rate does the marginal social benefit of labor equal the marginal social cost of labor?
17. What does the marginal social benefit equal when the L_2 units of labor are employed?
18. What does the marginal social cost equal when the L_2 units of labor are employed?
19. If L_2 units of labor are hired in this labor market, is the market efficient? (yes, no, can't tell)
20. If L_2 units of labor are employed in this labor market, what needs to happen to the number of laborers hired in order to obtain greater efficiency? (increase, decrease, no change)

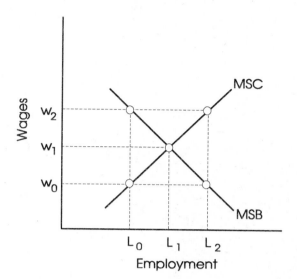

Labor Markets--Competitive and Noncompetitive

Use this figure to answer the following questions.

21. Which panel shows a firm operating in competitive labor and product markets?
22. Which panel shows a competitive firm (product market) with monopsony power?
23. In which panel does the VMP exceed the wage paid to workers by the greatest amount?
24. Which panel shows a firm with monopoly power that hires from a competitive labor market?
25. In which panel does MRP = VMP = w = MFC?

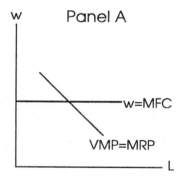

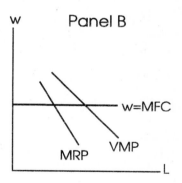

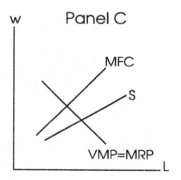

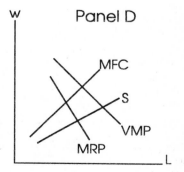

Answers for HomeWork Set II-9

(a) 1	(a) 28	(a) no change	(a) Area A
(b) 2	(b) 38	(b) excess supply	(b) Area B
(c) 3	(c) attend college	(c) MR = MC	(c) Area C
(d) 4	(d) start work after high school	(d) MRP = MFC	(d) w_0
(e) 5	(e) be a slacker	(e) D = S	(e) w_1

(a) 6	(a) the firm	(a) Panel A	(a) w_2
(b) 7	(b) the market	(b) Panel B	(b) yes
(c) 14	(c) workers	(c) Panel C	(c) no
(d) 18	(d) increase	(d) Panel D	(d) can't tell
(e) 20	(e) decrease	(e) Panels A-D	(e) perhaps

HomeWork Set II-10
Environmental Economics and Public Choice
(Chapters 18 & 19)

Externalities

Use this figure to answer the following questions. Output Qa is the market determined output in each panel.

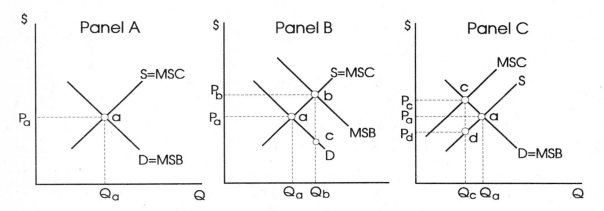

1. Which panel illustrates a market with no externalities?
2. Which panel illustrates a market in which external benefits or positive externalities are present?
3. In the panel where external costs are present, what is the efficient level of output? (Qa, Qb, or Qc)
4. If external costs are present, attaining an efficient output level through government action should cause market price to? (increase or decrease)
5. Which panel illustrates a market price that is less than MSB?
6. Which panel illustrates a market price that is less than MSC?

Assume panel C correctly models the current market outcome (assume also that the market is initially in equilibrium with no government intervention).

7. What type of government intervention will most likely move the market towards efficiency? (tax, or subsidy)
8. Which distance measures the size of the externality in panel C? (dc, ac, ad, or Qa-Qc)
9. In which panel does the market underestimate the true social costs of producing the good?
10. How large of a subsidy would be required to encourage the market with positive externalities to produce the socially optimal output? (ab, ac, cd, cb)

Pollution Abatement

Use this figure concerning pollution abatement to answer the following questions.

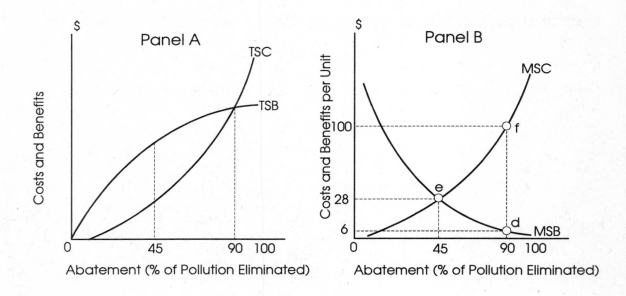

11. Under the conditions given in the figure, what is the optimal level of pollution abatement (in percent)?
12. At 45 % pollution abatement, how does the slope of the Total Social Cost (TSC) curve compare to the slope of the Total Social Benefit (TSB) curve? (equal to, greater than, or less than)
13. What does the distance between the TSC and the TSB curve measure? (net benefit, total benefit, or total cost of abatement)
14. What is the MSC (in dollars) of reducing pollution by 90%?
15. What is the MSB (in dollars) of reducing pollution by 90%?
16. Would it be efficient to reduce pollution by 90% under current conditions? (yes or no)
17. If pollution is reduced by 90%, what does the area def measure? (TSC, TSB, net benefit, or net loss)
18. How does one determine the optimal level of pollution abatement? (TSB = TSC, MSB = MSC, or S = D)

Voting Systems

Use the table below, which lists the benefits and costs of a proposed sewer system to the citizens of Centerville, to answer the following questions.

	Benefits	Costs	Points
Lynn	450	500	6
Mike	600	500	12
Diana	675	500	16
Norbert	400	500	12
Marla	475	500	3

19. If unanimity is required, will the initiative (proposed sewer system) pass? (yes or no)
20. If majority voting is used, will the initiative pass? (yes or no)
21. Will the outcome of majority voting be efficient? (yes or no)

Assume a point voting system is used and that each individual decides to allocate the points shown in the points column of the table.

22. How many points will the for side receive?
23. How many points will the against side receive?
24. Will the initiative pass? (yes or no)
25. Will the outcome of point voting be efficient? (yes or no)

Answers for HomeWork Set II-10

(a) 0	(a) ac	(a) tax	(a) TSC
(b) 6	(b) ad	(b) subsidy	(b) TSB
(c) 9	(c) Qa-Qc	(c) TSB = TSC	(c) equal to
(d) 18	(d) Qa	(d) MSB = MSC	(d) greater than
(e) 21	(e) Qb	(e) D = S	(e) less than

(a) 28	(a) Qc	(a) Panel A	(a) ab
(b) 45	(b) net benefit	(b) Panel B	(b) cb
(c) 90	(c) net loss	(c) Panel C	(c) Q_b
(d) 100	(d) total benefit	(d) increase	(d) yes
(e) dc	(e) total cost	(e) decrease	(e) no

NOTES

NOTES

NOTES

NOTES

NOTES

NOTES

NOTES

NOTES

NOTES